Your Profile

Professional career coaching

John Lowe

A Lowe Publication™

Text © John Lowe, 2010.

The right of John Lowe to be identified as author of this work has been asserted by him in accordance with the Copyright, Designs and Patents Act 1988.

No other rights are granted without permission in writing from the publisher.

Copy by any other means or for any other purpose is strictly prohibited without the prior written consent of the copyright holders.

Application for such permission should be addressed to the publisher. Published in 2010 by:

**Regent eLearning Limited
Linen Hall, 162 Regent Street
London, W1B 5TG
United Kingdom**

ISBN: 978-1-907824-00-5

Layout and illustrations by Giorgio Giussani.

Edited by Judi Hunter.

Printed in Great Britain by TJ International Ltd.

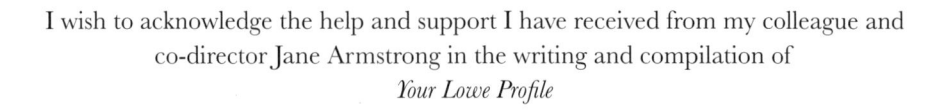

■ ■ ■

I wish to acknowledge the help and support I have received from my colleague and co-director Jane Armstrong in the writing and compilation of
Your Lowe Profile

What others say...

John Lowe gave me valuable support and advice during the lengthy process of selection, training and qualifying as a medical doctor. I shall refer to Your Lowe Profile *as an expert career reference manual when I must choose the GP or consultancy route. The positive 'can do' tone is motivational for anyone in whatever employment.*

Dr Lauren Trisk

This coaching programme made me more aware of my core strengths and provided me with a universal 'tool' that I can use whenever I want to successfully present myself. I have a stronger self-awareness – and it has really worked for me as I now have an attractive job offer!

Nadine Vieker MBA
Judge Business School Strategy Consultant, University of Cambridge

The interview and coaching instruction was invaluable for me – not only did it focus me on my key strengths, but it provided me with a clear and simple platform to deliver these. I felt that my ability to perform was significantly enhanced and I would certainly recommend Your Lowe Profile *to my colleagues. I felt that it also enhanced my own skills and understanding of myself.*

Charlie Sim
Marketing Consultant, Cap Gemini Consulting

Your Lowe Profile *gives the reader practical and applicable tools for career development and success at work. The sections on understanding 'self' and personalising a winning profile for interviews and meetings are uniquely insightful.*

Dr Graham Davies
FRSA, Fellow Commoner, Sidney Sussex College, University of Cambridge

This is an excellent book which summarises the guidance John has given to MBA students at some of the UK's top business schools, not to mention countless practising managers and senior executives. If you want a high-profile career, Your Lowe Profile *is a very good primer for preparing your job search, CV development and interview technique. I know it works as I have used it successfully myself.*

Dr Huw Morris
Dean, MMU Business School

John Lowe has provided consistent and personal support as I navigated my career from successful qualification through the early years of clinical practice and into the broad future ahead of me. I will use Your Lowe Profile *as a permanent reference and guide for career-related decisions.*

Dr Stephanie Johnson

I have thoroughly enjoyed reading your book and can of course relate to all you say, having been a member of your club for several years now.

I confirm that your style and approach has been effective for me.

I am happy to use your words as you have been all that for me – 'a permanent and comprehensive expert coach for personal and career development'.

Simon Manasseh
General Manager, Western Harvesters (CLAAS)

Your Lowe Profile *is an impressive and instructive piece. There is clearly an eager audience out there who will benefit greatly from its contents and my only regret is that it wasn't available when I was struggling to find work. Mind you, John's personal coaching was a very good substitute!*

Edward Brunel-Cohen
Global Head of Finance, Chartered Institute for Securities and Investment

John is very good at ensuring that he does not make decisions for you but steers you along the decision-making path – a path which had become rather confused for me!

Your Lowe Profile provides all the advice, guidance and expert knowledge that John has acquired in a concise but very warm and friendly format. Your Lowe Profile provides detail on personality profiles, CV styling and interview technique that will allow an individual, regardless of the career they are pursuing, to make the next brave steps forward. I am in a job where I am challenged, rewarded and most importantly absolutely love.

Jake Armstrong
Secondary School Teacher

The appendices on listening skills and, in particular, stress, relative to the four personality types, is insightful and highly relevant to today's business environment. By helping the reader understand their own personality type and how that relates to others in a work scenario, Your Lowe Profile has provided a structured and sequential approach to job selection, winning at interview and performing in the role. Your Lowe Profile is required reading for anyone, irrespective of their job type or professional status, who may be seeking practical, real-world guidance on how to identify, secure and excel in their chosen field.

Adam Smith
Business Consultant

Thank you so much for your time once again! Your advice at the sessions I've had with you and your team since completing my MBA and during the programme have been invaluable. I think my success at both interviews I have attended was in large part due to the preparation techniques.

You might be interested to know that I am in touch with several of my fellow alumni who feel the same about your coaching programme.

Vivian Davies
MBA Durham

You managed to explain sometimes rather complicated psychological facts in a very short, simple and easy-to-understand way. The logical sequence of chapter contents and the fact that each chapter can be read in its own right, or rather re-read to refresh the memory in case of need, shows your professional experience with the topic. Your language is clear and specific and you manage to keep the unavoidable repetitions to make the individual chapters readable in their own right to a minimum.

I found the sub chapter 'Responding to job advertisements' absolutely outstanding. It provides such a wealth of advice, which sounds logical when reading it but does not come naturally to the inexperienced applicant, and it also shows your extraordinary experience in the subject. I have never seen anything similar before. This chapter alone makes buying and reading the book worthwhile for any job seeker!

Your analysis, advice and your tips for the interviewing practice are all very valuable know-how to any manager. I wish I had the book when I was interviewing, as I did it mostly structured only around historical data and hard job-related facts not knowing how to sensibly tackle the soft aspects. Likewise, your advice in the appendices will provide useful thoughts to all ambitious and even experienced professionals. It must be rewarding to pass on this wealth of experience and know-how in a rather specific topic to the wider professional public.

Uwe Muller
Former Managing Director, Siemens Power Generation

Contents

Introduction _____ 11

    About the author _____ 12

    The work environment and you _____ 14

    Today's work climate _____ 15

    Managing change _____ 17

Chapter 1 Your Personality Profile _____ 18

    Building your personality profile _____ 19

    The Supporter _____ 20

    The Influencer _____ 24

    The Creative _____ 28

    The Analyst _____ 32

    The Creative type is overlooked _____ 36

    You are not born a leader _____ 36

    Now I know my personality _____ 38

Chapter 2 Your Job Profile _____ 40

    The market today _____ 40

    Building your job profile _____ 40

    Part 1 Personal preferences _____ 41

    Part 2 Personal circumstances _____ 46

    Parts 3 and 4 Soft skills and personal experience ____ 47

    Part 5 Remuneration _____ 49

    Your Job Profiler _____ 51

The benefits of building your job profile	52
Writing a successful CV	53
CV composition	58
Finding the job	63

Chapter 3 Your Interview Profile — 82

What is an interview?	82
Your Interview Profiler	83
Your strengths	84
Compiling Your Interview Profiler	85
Using Your Interview Profiler in the interview	89

Chapter 4 Your Work Profile — 92

Your personality at work	93
Meetings	94
Progress review meeting – annual appraisals	102
There is more to know...	103

Appendices — 104

Listening skills	104
Stress	107
Interviewing candidates	111
Career goal setting	114

Introduction

Your Lowe Profile offers you an expert reference to successfully manage the core and critical events that will challenge you throughout your working life. Needing a positive job change or the prospect of redundancy will no longer present itself as an occasion for concern, rather a situation of opportunity.

Learning how to identify your real personality strengths, knowing what is your ideal job role, always powerfully performing at interview and consistently achieving top performance at work is the exciting journey of discovery upon which you are about to embark.

About the author

I have coached in excess of 20,000 candidates from virtually every industry. Headhunting and coaching are normally viewed as separate disciplines, but I believe they are interdependent. Because I am also a headhunter, I am able to coach a candidate more effectively as I know the job market and therefore their potential career growth, their opportunities and their realistic salary expectations.

I coach leading university professors, Senior Board Managing Directors, candidates requiring help in degree choice and university selection, executives wishing to improve their career focus and MBA students seeking personal development and career advice. This range of experience is unusual in the market as most coaches tend to concentrate on particular segments, but I have found my extensive and broad knowledge-base advantageous in that it allows me to give more qualitative and contextual advice.

This range of experience is important to endorse. Large corporations, for example, present a different dynamic and structure to new start-ups. Politics can play an important role within large multinationals and influence the determination of its processes, procedures and administration, all factors that are critical to its successful operation. Start-ups, on the other hand, require a mentality of initiative, creativity and an element of risk taking. Each industry will have its own unique dynamic and atmosphere that superimposes a further variant within the work environment.

Medicine, law, accounting, oil, banking, PR, advertising, design, consultancy, charities, architecture, manufacturing, IT, telecoms and retail all have commercial criteria that are unique to their activity. *Your Lowe Profile* incorporates this diversity within its coaching and uniquely delivers instructional profilers that you can universally apply to any industry. *Your Lowe Profile* equips you with the skills to cope with predictable and unpredictable eventualities. It replicates the reality of today's employment markets.

You will be introduced to a constructive and structured approach that will equip you with all the necessary knowledge and skills to confidently find that ideal challenge in terms of role responsibility and remuneration. This book will help you to find that ideal role by introducing you to a logical and positive career finding path. No matter what the circumstances, whether a promotion, a new career, an annual appraisal, redundancy or a lifestyle change, you will be challenged and energised and emerge feeling confident about yourself, your strengths and your ability to present yourself positively.

I have compiled this coaching manual in a logical sequence in terms of chronology and I have written each section so that it will stand alone. This will enable you to refer to a specific subject or topic separately and independently. You can therefore use it as an expert reference for planned or unforeseen career-related events or situations such as headhunts, redundancy and interviews.

The content will not change over time. I have applied these techniques for more than 35 years to the UK, European and world markets. The techniques are people, not culture, specific.

The work environment and you

How well do you know yourself? How would you describe your personality? Are you often misunderstood? Is introvert good? Is extrovert better? Do you crave to be the life and soul of the party or would you prefer to read a good book?

'They would say that, wouldn't they?'

'That remark seems out of character!'

'He's a character!'

These personality-related comments will be familiar to you. Most people's aspirations are to be 'in character', but can we ever know our real personality and our strong points? Could we apply that knowledge to the job market? We all have different aspirations and want to gain something different from our working day. Uniquely and sequentially, *Your Lowe Profile* will show you how to do just that.

Today's market is focused on the short term. The work environment is ever changing and there is a greater turnover of people in job roles.

Throughout your working life you will meet situations that are planned and predictable. You will also find yourself in situations that are spontaneous and unscheduled. *Your Lowe Profile* will teach you to proactively and reactively manage these situations successfully.

The employment market constantly uses the word 'skills' as core terminology and an explanation of its meaning might help here. The term has two categories: soft and technical. Soft skills refer to personality traits such as good communicator, industrious, reliable, flexible, ambitious and determined. Technical skills are acquired through training and experience, and proficiency in a particular technical skill will be determined by the level of training received and how it is applied. Job descriptions and job adverts will specify the skills required and use the term 'skill' in both the soft and technical contexts.

Your Lowe Profile will help you to become more successful by revealing and refining your talents and skills and showing you how to apply them effectively within the work environment. The style of the book is such that it will engage with you individually.

Your Lowe Profile treats you as an individual and uniquely combines the changing work environment with your special skills. Foundational to these skills are four personality types, which I will identify. These will help you to understand through self-validation your personality profile and what it means in a work situation. We often read famous VIP or celebrity profiles. These profiles describe the celebrity's personality and their history. 'Profile' is regarded as an inclusive term, incorporating character traits and actions past and present. Throughout your working life, you will constantly have to manage one or more of these critical stages:

Your job profile *your adaptation to the ever-changing environment.*

Your interview profile *your performance during assessments.*

Your work profile *your achievements at work.*

I chose the title of this book purposefully. Profiling your dominant personality characteristics and contextually applying them to career management will mean you have expert coaching advice for ready reference, which you can consult in order to manage your critical life stages positively. Using my own name emphasises the fact that this new material and its structured presentation is based on my first-hand research and experience.

Today's work climate

The present working environment, whether it is a commercially-focused corporation or a not-for-profit organisation, is demanding and has a short-term cycle. It will be influenced by the short-term trading culture that is so prevalent in today's market.

Influencers such as global markets, off-shoring, employee mobility, technology growth, interest rates, booms, recessions, credit crunches, wars and global warming collectively and interactively create an ongoing and dynamic change in world economies.

A significant new development in today's commercial environment is the fact that work or the task takes priority over the people factor.

Historically, many large corporations had a strong people-focused culture. To ensure promotion, employees would endeavour to establish strong positive associations with influencing managers. Companies' paternalistic attitude to their employees and the employment benefit package reflected this with subsidised luncheons, education subsidies, generous pensions and an active policy of ongoing training and development. The general culture was such that if an employee made a request that would enhance their career prospects, then that request would be positively considered.

Fundamentally, that culture has changed and because of the pressure to 'do it now' the dynamic has developed from a predominately people emphasis to a job or task priority – the job rules.

Have you done it? When will it be ready? How are you getting on with that project? Are we within time? Are we within budget? These questions replicate a modern pressurised workplace. They have replaced a dialogue that used to be more people centric.

No matter what stage we are at in life, we would each like to improve ourselves and develop further. The purpose of *Your Lowe Profile* is to act as an expert reference point throughout your commercial life on all topics concerning your personal development and career management. The topics will include the identification of your personality strengths and how to apply this knowledge successfully.

How do you know what your ideal job role is? Where do you find it and how do you apply for it? How can you ensure that you present yourself positively and successfully at all interviews? How can you do your job better and improve your performance at work?

The objective is to make you more aware of your unique talents and skills and how and where you should best apply them. If you have wonderful presentation skills, use them. If you have special technical skills, apply them.

Being in the wrong job can make you feel stressed, frustrated, depressed and adopt a negative attitude. In the right job, you will feel positive, motivated and enthusiastic and be good to be with. Jobs have an enormous influence on the quality of our life. The time you spend following my coaching advice will have real and positive benefits.

Managing change

The rate of change in the modern commercial environment means we may cross a number of career boundaries during our working life. We need to be able to adapt to this rate of change and adjust to different work situations. This book will give you the skills to do this.

Career advice is a subject on which you will find an amazing array of material, incorporating a wide range of suggestions that can be contradictory or sound good on paper but are difficult to apply. Employees are frequently sent on courses that focus on change management and work processes. My emphasis is the reverse of this. I believe it is more productive to give priority to coaching the individual to recognise their particular skills and strengths, which they can then apply to real work situations as they change.

High-performing athletes will receive individual coaching to achieve high levels of performance within their particular sport. The main emphasis is on improving their skills to best deal tactically with the race or game, which by its nature is an unpredictable event. *Your Lowe Profile* endorses the same philosophy. The time spent on personal skills development is more productive than time spent on theoretically studying an unpredictable event. Many of the leading business schools have acknowledged this modern trend and are incorporating these skills as an integral part of their MBA courses. I am personally assisting leading universities in their development work to achieve that objective.

Identifying your particular individual personality type and your strengths enables you to manage situations effectively and successfully. *Your Lowe Profile* has a positive tone. It capitalises only on your strengths. It does not ignore your weaknesses. If you are a world class sprinter, you do not enter marathons.

In Chapter 1, I look at the psychology of personality and help you to identify your particular personality type and how you relate it to a work environment. This is in contrast to a social environment, where telling risqué jokes and being the 'life and soul of the party' may be viewed positively by your friends but not regarded as suitable behaviour in a business presentation. That is not to say that the work environment should not be fun, allowing for a good sense of humour, but, contextually, the focus is different – ultimately you are there to achieve business goals.

Each year we grow in experience within an ever-changing environment. *Your Lowe Profile* will ensure that knowledgeably and attitudinally you embrace that change and use it always to enhance your performance and achieve your career goals.

Chapter 1 Your Personality Profile

This is an exciting chapter where you will learn more about yourself by identifying your personality profile, and how you behave and are perceived in a working environment. How you react to others on a one-to-one or group basis will be influenced and determined by your corporate persona (personality at work). Identifying your personality characteristics and understanding others will help you to cope better with people dynamics and more productively manage and influence situations at work.

My experience of interviewing and coaching has identified four personality types:

- **The Supporter.**
- **The Influencer.**
- **The Creative.**
- **The Analyst.**

We all have these traits in different measures.

The Supporter and the Influencer are predominately 'people oriented' in their behaviour. This means that their emphasis is to consider the people implications first and then the task.

The Creative and the Analyst are predominately 'task oriented' in their behaviour. This means that they focus firstly on the task and then on the people factors.

The four personality types are innate and have individual personality traits and characteristics. Your personality does not normally change, though you will frequently modify your behaviour to conform to situations. You may consider yourself to be a shy person, but enjoy giving a prepared presentation to a public group.

From my experience, most people will have a dominant and a secondary trait that influence their behaviour.

Every individual will possess a degree of all four characteristics. When I am interviewing or coaching candidates, they find it fascinating as we discuss their dominant trait and its implications. Conducting an analysis of their career to date and demonstrating how their performance and skills historically match and are facilitated by their traits as I define them, tends to be a revelatory road of discovery for them. The coaching facilitates future informed career choices.

This self-help and self-validated type of testing and the opportunity to make a self-analysis of your personal strengths is unique in the market. The personal validation makes it practical, usable and highly relevant to today's work climate. Use it and gain the benefit.

This group and descriptor of types is based on my personal analysis of the many thousands of one-to-one interviews I conduct when I have the unique opportunity of contextually assessing and categorising behaviours, and thereby develop psychological models.

Building your personality profile

To help you to identify your dominant personality profile, I have described the psychological characteristics of each type, including their management style and how they interact with each other.

Some people are predominately one type, whilst others will be a combination of types. There is no golden rule. The types pre-empt behaviours which, when applied in a commercial environment, will help you to better understand how you should interact at work in relation to people and tasks. It will help you to understand why, historically, you did not enjoy certain work tasks and, conversely, why you were so successful in fulfilling certain roles.

Read the descriptions of the four personality types on pages 20–35 and discover your dominant and secondary characteristics.

Self-validation and evaluation is always difficult. Be as objective as possible and refer to historical events as a benchmark for evaluation. For example, if you organised a charity event, what were the aspects you enjoyed the most – the people interaction, achieving a high level of donations, or perhaps enjoying the benefits the fund made to a particular worthwhile cause?

In order to help you to apply your personality type to the work environment, I have included a paragraph at the end of each type that is a summation of your particular skills. These summaries can be applied to Chapter 2 Your Job Profile which coaches you in 'finding the job'.

The Supporter

In common parlance, the Supporter could be described as a 'people person'. They are good judges of character and have a strong ability to empathise with others. In terms of the corporate environment, the Supporter likes to display the following characteristics:

- Enjoys helping people and gaining recognition for doing so.

- Engages with colleagues on a meaningful and personal basis.

- Will support weaker members of a team and help them to develop.

- Empathetic and sensitive to others – strong aptitude for customer care and client services.

- Dislikes confrontation and does not voluntarily interact with truculent, domineering types.

- A tendency to be over concerned regarding the sensitivities of colleagues and to lose focus in terms of commercial objectives.

The strong people aspect of their personality will mean that their judgements and comments will be from the people perspective. Their descriptions will focus on the players rather than the game, the actors rather than the film, the personnel rather than the project.

Descriptive lexicon

trainer	caring	intuitive	good communicator
instructor	good listener	adaptable	compliant
coach	co-operative	compassionate	collaborative
mentor	patient	team player	conformist
sympathetic	tolerant	trustworthy	positive
friendly	honest	reliable	unselfish
empathetic	sensitive	thoughtful	sincere
flexible	stable		

Management style

The Supporter will encourage the collaborative approach and would prefer everybody to be in agreement and willingly conform. They will have difficulty managing the aggressive non-co-operative type who endeavours to undermine their credibility and authority. They will need to 'step out' of character and depersonalise the situation by exclusively focusing on the task in order to manage the non-conformist type successfully.

They are a popular leader and their non-confrontational style means people feel included. Ensuring that everyone is happy and motivated is the Supporter's goal. Achieving power or boosting their own ego is not their driver, and their modest management approach can be an effective recipe for successful leadership.

The Supporter and their interactions

The Supporter views situations from the people perspective. They are good judges of character and will understand and empathise with people's strengths, weaknesses, concerns and problems. They will be influenced by people's mood. If their friends are happy, they will want to join them and share their joy or good news.

Supporters are good team builders. They can choose different types to complement a working environment. They 'get on well' together. They 'like' each other. Their comments about people will be emotionally based. Supporters are sensitive and do not like truculent, aggressive types whom they will avoid, interacting only when necessary.

The Supporter will remember the office birthdays. They will buy the card and ensure colleagues sign it; when staff are leaving, they will organise the collection and buy the present.

At work and as a manager, they will be predominantly people oriented and will adopt a style that believes strongly in the premise that a happy team is a productive team and a work/life balance is a positive career goal.

In the commercial environment, Supporters need to constantly modify and reaffirm their focus to see their duties and responsibilities in a task and goal oriented form, rather than based predominantly on 'people interactions' with obscurely defined commercial objectives.

Supporters are moody and enjoy sharing their feelings with others. They are loyal, reliable and honest and will not voluntarily interact with people who are unreliable, dishonest and, in their mind, lacking the most fundamental characteristic if they are to be their friend – integrity.

It is important that the Supporter feels valued by their employer. Recognition for good effort will ensure that the Supporter is highly motivated and committed. Trust is one of the Supporter's highest values. If you are a friend, they will expect that trust to be reciprocated. If you break that trust, the Supporter may ostracise you as a friend and you will have difficulty regaining that confidence.

Supporter > Supporter

This results in a really happy conversational 'marriage'. Both natures are kindly, unselfish and generous. You can imagine them swapping presents when they meet. Their conversations will be people focused, especially with friends and colleagues at work. They enjoy office politics and their kindly nature will manifest itself particularly when they are discussing members of staff. Supporters enjoy each other's company. Those whom they might dislike will be given the 'benefit of the doubt' for selfish actions and the Supporter is apologetic if they feel they have or may have caused any offence. They will worry until the situation is rectified.

Supporter > Influencer

The Supporter enjoys the company of an Influencer who also has a predominately people orientation. The Supporter enjoys the fact that the Influencer is open, talkative and emotionally transparent. The Influencer is more self-centred than the Supporter would like, but their openness compensates and the Supporter will keep the Influencer in their phone book and invite them to a party because they will liven up the event.

Supporter > Creative

Mindful that the Supporter's primary focus is people, the Supporter will judge a new logo or marketing strap line from the originator's perspective. If they know and like the artist, the logo design will be appreciated sympathetically. If they do not know the originator, they are inclined to ask questions about context, objective and circumstances of the work before making an opinion. Supporters are not naturally critical and this sympathetic and empathetic attitude is positively appreciated by Creatives.

Supporter > Analyst

This makes for a difficult relationship. 'They are too quiet.' 'I don't know what they're thinking.' The verbally reclusive nature of the Analyst is a real challenge for the Supporter as this person does not enter the emotional, talkative arena where the Supporter can engage with them. 'Let your hair down.' 'You are very uptight.' 'Show your emotions, for goodness sake!' This is what the Supporter would like to tell the Analyst.

Supporter – career skills

The Supporter is highly adaptable and can relate well to colleagues and technologies. When you are endeavouring to search job advertisements, you may find you have a wide choice. To refine your choice, follow these recommendations. The people contact should be in the context of training, helping, instructing or leading. Avoid roles that involve overt selling skills – this is ideally the Influencer's domain.

Whilst the duties and responsibilities of a role are important to all of us, you will find that a friendly collaborative working atmosphere will be most motivational. You will benefit from the team environment and perform better within this structure. Avoid roles that are isolationist and do not require people engagement. Doctors, nurses, lawyers and accountants can be Supporters and the majority of functional roles in most organisations will have Supporters as the most popular personality characteristic. So your choice is comprehensive.

Your major challenge will be following the advice above regarding the atmosphere criteria. To find out how well you might fit into the team, you can only really decide after your interview or when you have worked in the environment for some weeks. Do, therefore, pay particular attention to the detail of the advertisement and, whilst on interview, ask searching questions in terms of the people interaction aspect of the role. Refer to your descriptive lexicon and look for advertisements that emphasise these skills: good communicator, team player, flexible, reliable, trainer, instructor, etc.

The Influencer

The Influencer is articulate and outgoing and may be described as being 'a good talker'. They are likely to display the following qualities:

- Outgoing and verbose with an answer for everything.

- Enjoys the social aspect of the work environment. Has a wide circle of friends and dislikes 'sitting in'.

- Always shares their opinions and experiences with others.

- A good leader whom others find inspirational.

- A strong negotiator and sales person.

- Likely to dominate group meetings.

- Highly political in a work environment.

An Influencer has good commercial acumen and can be motivated by the prospect of earning commission or a bonus based on performance. They will endeavour to take up promotion opportunities and, consequently, can move up the career ladder faster. A higher income also gives them the option to indulge in 'good taste' for expensive purchases.

Descriptive lexicon

lively	resourceful	positive	commercially aware
engaging	motivational	decisive	strong communicator
articulate	competitive	poor listener	target driven
fun	vigorous	witty	results orientated
challenging	energetic	convincing	sociable
inspiring	spontaneous	adventurous	believable

Management style

The Influencer's style best suits sales teams where inspirational and positive encouragement is needed. They may have difficulty leading technical teams whereby they may need to adopt a more consensual approach, concentrating on rationale and task goals, rather than emotive transient argument.

The Influencer enjoys the 'limelight' and being the focus of attention. They enjoy compliments and positive feedback. 'Great speech!' 'Best presentation I have heard for years!' These reputation-enhancing comments will delight the Influencer who has the unique skill to adapt their management style to suit the audience. The Influencer is a purveyor of good news and a natural leader with a very positive disposition.

The Influencer and their interactions

The Influencer, like the Supporter, has a predominant people orientation. They enjoy people interaction, but will have less people empathy than a Supporter. They most often manifest an extrovert personality. They have a propensity to adjust their behaviour to suit the situation.

The Influencer is extremely flexible and adaptable and will endeavour to establish a positive rapport with their manager. They recognise corporate hierarchy and can be relied upon to get a job done. Their positive mindset/ego is their driver.

If they produce a great performance, the Influencer expects a great response: 'You were great.' 'That's the best!' 'Congratulations!' 'How did you do that?' 'Oh, it was nothing,' is their polite response as they gloat in the adulation. The Influencer has a positive disposition and is a good talker. The natural flipside to being a good talker is being a poor listener.

'Let me tell you about the bargain I got on eBay. Can anyone guess how much I paid for these?' Whether anyone is interested in the items, their value or how much the Influencer paid are not factors that would be remotely considered by the Influencer. If challenged conversationally, they will sternly defend their position.

The Influencer's large ego does not allow much room for modesty. Their predominant work pattern is to perform and manage through verbal influence. If colleagues are reluctant to co-operate, the Influencer will engage verbally and 'sell' the idea.

Influencers are strong time managers but poor at assimilating detail. 'It's the big picture that counts,' will be their energetic philosophy. Identifying the core facts can be a challenge to the Influencer, as the premise of 'how I say it' can be more persuasive than 'what I say'.

A striking presentation may have to sacrifice content and detail and, therefore, the Influencer may apply embellishment and exaggeration to persuade the audience. This is acceptable behaviour from their perspective, providing the audience is not misled and the substance is true.

They are self-centred and enjoy sharing their ideas. They enjoy lively debate and challenging other opinions, raising the tempo by expressing controversial and non-conformist viewpoints. Influencers are likeable, positive, active, have a good sense of humour and a 'can do' mentality.

The Influencer may become lazy if their work does not motivate them. They are easily bored and will move jobs more often than most. Money, variety and challenge are their drivers and they will aim to achieve targets and receive commission. Their vocabulary is often supercharged with emotive terms.

'Life and soul of the party' is a good description and whether at a party or at work the Influencer will be very interested in what people do. Status is important to the Influencer.

Influencer > Supporter

The Supporter is the Influencer's favourite type who also understands and likes people. The Influencer can persuade the Supporter to conform to their way of thinking. The Supporter is considered to be great company, a good friend and provide a good listening platform, without challenge or interruption.

Influencer > Influencer

This is an interesting interaction. Basically, we have two talkative, poor listening types who will vie for the dominant position on the verbal stage. 'You are not listening to a word I am saying,' might be a fair reflection of both their reactions. They are both competitive with large egos and their interactions tend to have lots of boastful content. A lively mix; talking at rather than to each other best describes this engagement.

Influencer > Creative

The Influencer does not empathise with the Creative as the Creative is not a predominately people person. Discussing the intricacies of people's personalities for its own sake is a meaningless exercise to the Creative. They need common ground, such as Picasso's personality and behaviour and how this influenced his artistic work. Expressing unsubstantiated and spontaneous remarks about a revered artwork will not match the Creative's deeper sense of appreciation.

Influencer > Analyst

We might refer to this as a clash of personalities. The Influencer's conversation will most often be people or personality centric, which will not have much appeal to the Analyst who engages mostly on the basis of facts and information. The Influencer will consider the Analyst to be too quiet and difficult to engage with in conversation, as the Influencer will not obtain any feedback in terms of emotional reaction.

Influencer – career skills

Look for a role with a high level of people interaction whereby you have the opportunity to persuade, sell and influence. There should be scope to earn fees or bonuses based on your own success. The product or service you are promoting should not be too technical, as you will only be happy presenting the 'big picture' rather than the minutiae. The selling cycle should not be too protracted. Long-term negotiations normally involve complicated product or service specification and will not offer a productive platform for the Influencer to apply their strong persuasive skills. You will be capable of selling on a one-to-one basis, to groups and to senior Boards. The greater the audience, the more you will rise to the challenge. You enjoy variety in terms of dealing with different clients and also in terms of location. You should not just be office bound.

Look for jobs with the following components:

- People contact – to persuade, to influence.
- Service/product – not too technical – which can be effectively introduced and described via a presentation or on an individual basis.
- Variety – different clients, different location.
- Financial reward based on performance.

Pay particular attention to advertisements where the following skills are highlighted: strong communicator, results orientated, commission/bonus paid on results, target driven, challenging, motivator, decisive.

The Creative

The Creative is a lateral Analyst with the ability to think 'outside the square' and bring a fresh, original perspective to workplace challenges. The following characteristics are typical of the Creative:

- A creative aptitude, which can manifest as a special design talent or a strong appreciation of the arts.

- Takes nothing for granted.

- Enjoys new ideas and non-traditional routes to problem solving.

- Confidently states opinions on advertising campaigns, market trends and future product and lifestyle developments.

- Over sensitive at times and does not take criticism well.

- Has difficulties with time management and works on the philosophy of 'Give me more time and I can do an even better job.'

- Has 3D visualisation.

Descriptive lexicon

interesting	adventurous	expressive	pioneering
unconventional	visualiser	industrious	creative
conscientious	demanding	analytical	designer
optimistic	efficient	a 'can do' attitude	conceptual
talented	deliberate	organised	judgemental
good listener			

Management style

The Creative adopts a fast-forward 'follow me' style of management. They strive to achieve optimum standards and will expect the same aspirant attitude from their team. The nuances of office politics will present a particular challenge to the Creative, who should ignore such distracting permutations and retain their strong focus on the commercial goals. The Creative is a strong, non-political, no-nonsense leader whose natural enthusiasm creates a positive effective management style. They dislike criticism and can appear opinionated and autocratic in their approach, but the corollary to this style is the fact that they know where they are going and how they are going to get there.

The Creative and their interactions

The Creative has an amazing ability to visualise conceptually from many perspectives. They create designs relating to architecture, products, fashion and packaging; write books, plays, lyrics, advertising jingles; paint, illustrate; compose, perform, etc. – creations that have underpinned the worldwide success of some of our best-known products, art, architecture, music, advertising and fashion.

The Creative can be opinionated and stubborn and will generally defend any criticism of their work.

When I am describing personality types, I am predominantly describing the trait or characters in isolation and outlining the main or predominant behaviours for that particular type. Picasso, Yehudi Menuhin and Andrew Lloyd-Webber manifest unique creative talents.

The Creative has a talent that they must have the scope to manifest or apply. The architect must design. The artist must paint. The Creative has a strong talent for design and they are motivated when they are positively developing and applying that talent within a practical application.

The Creative is open and transparent in their views and will enjoy intellectualising discussions.

Creative > Supporter

These types will interact well due to the profile of the Supporter who will always demonstrate an interest in other people and their work.

Creative > Influencer

This is not an ideal 'marriage'. Mindful that the Creative is purposeful in their thoughts and practical in their application, these are restrictions that the Influencer does not enjoy. The Creative is essentially not a people person and hence may not be on the same 'wavelength' as the talkative, ebullient Influencer.

Creative > Creative

The Creative type, like the Analyst, is task focused and interacts well as they can normally identify a topic for discussion. Being highly imaginative and creative, they are interested in each other's opinion and perspective on design topics. They are active, conversational participants and enjoy each other's company – a good match.

Creative > Analyst

The Creative will engage well with the Analyst. Both types are predominately task driven rather than people orientated. They both focus on the detail and facts of situations rather than hyperbole.

Creative – career skills

The Creative should seek only roles where there is scope to apply their talent. This can be in many forms. You may be designing, composing, writing, painting, commissioning or briefing designers, studio managing or you may be project managing the creative processes ensuring brand integrity and brief compliance. You may seek roles to apply your own creative specialism or, as a manager, to brief the creative team.

You may enjoy manifesting your creative skills in the field of literature, music or the fine arts, or you may apply your unique talent to the more functional attributes of daily life. Design skills are latent or overt in all products we use – cars, furniture, houses, interiors, offices, mobiles, computers and packaging. Creativity is a unique skill and whatever your experience and seniority, whether you are seeking a junior, middleweight or director level role, you should always ensure that there is a design or creative component compatible with your ideal career aspiration and talent. Otherwise, you will feel frustrated and bored and compelled to seek a new opportunity.

The nature of the work should have strong, challenging and varied components. Creatives tend to change jobs more than average. Creative design assignments have definitive time spans and 'treading water' or waiting for the next challenge is not the Creative's normal or comfortable remit. Hence, working freelance on an assignment-by-assignment basis can suit well in terms of optimum application of skills.

When you are job hunting, you must decide whether you are seeking a role to demonstrate and apply your particular skills or whether you are seeking a role whereby you are facilitating third-party ideas and recommendations.

Look for advertisements describing the role as challenging, requiring a strong creative/design component and a positive proactive mentality. Look for roles with new unique challenges that do not contain repetitive boring elements.

The Analyst

The prevailing quality of the Analyst is the ability to approach and solve problems in a highly rational, structured manner. In terms of personality characteristics, the following are likely to apply:

- Enjoys the challenge of working things out independently.

- Enjoys problem solving – the greater the problem, the greater the challenge and the greater the intellectual satisfaction.

- Happier expressing facts over feelings.

- Lacks motivation if the task in hand is perceived to be pointless.

- Enjoys their own company.

- A good listener.

- Lacking in verbal spontaneity.

Descriptive lexicon

reliable	consistent	sceptical	tolerant
technical	independent	patient	analytical
thorough	stable	meticulous	adaptable
good listener	deliberate	thoughtful	determined
logical	accurate	problem solver	resilient
industrious			

Management style

The Analyst has a consensual rather than dictatorial style. They only ever follow reasoned debate and would therefore only expect to proffer the same respect to others. They are purposeful and not emotive whilst leading a group and, although the journey may not be the most inspirational or exciting experience for colleagues, Analysts have the reputation for achieving goals within the specified targets and will therefore drive their team hard if need be – they are tough task masters. Their style is a no-nonsense, philosophical approach, incorporating profundity in argument and never profuse. If people decide not to follow or co-operate, the Analyst will interpret their reaction in the context of being their prerogative and choice and not endeavour to influence it. This approach is unlike the Supporter or Influencer who will spend much time encouraging their colleagues to be always on-side.

The Analyst is a successful leader who will brief their team members thoroughly in terms of subject content and role.

The Analyst and their interactions

The Analyst is clinical in their judgements. They are not predominately people oriented and have a clear focus on the task in hand. Interestingly, during past recessions, more Analysts have been seen to be new business starters though they are not natural entrepreneurs. Historically, this was the Influencer's home territory.

For example, technology, not people, present scope for the Analyst to develop a new software tool and launch it via the internet. There is no face-to-face people sales contact. Their clever technology may identify and satisfy a market gap and need. The technology is also a non-people platform on which to market and launch. They can be today's new entrepreneurs. Think of the founders of the world's largest and most successful IT companies.

The Analyst can be considered introverted. They are thoughtful in response, rarely circumlocutory and only comment on what they know. The Analyst does not hold grudges and, if offended, reviews the situation circumspectly rather than personally, commenting something along the lines of, 'They would say that, wouldn't they?'

Analysts are not good time managers. They can be too fastidious in their work mentality, and when applying themselves to a task can supply a level of detail that was neither prescribed nor required.

Analyst > Supporter

The Analyst and Supporter can relate well and, due to their personality dispositions, they would rarely be at loggerheads. The Analyst is neither verbally aggressive nor pontifical and the Supporter is accommodating and kindly. So, whilst they may not have too much in common, they also have little 'out of common'.

Analyst > Influencer

The Analyst may ignore a lot of the content of the 'spontaneously articulate' Influencer. They consider the Influencer as talkative and technologically lightweight. They are basically two opposites. The Analyst thinks in terms of job/task and the Influencer thinks people first then task. Conversation based on highly speculative content does not interest the Analyst.

Analyst > Creative

These two types get on well. They are both task oriented and share an appreciation for numeracy, technology and science. The Analyst and Creative have much in common in their work ethic. They are conscientious, reliable and good at technical detail, and they are both primarily task focused.

Analyst > Analyst

You can envisage two scientists avidly discussing Stephen Hawking's *A Brief History of Time*. Conversely, if they do not identify a subject for common debate, the meeting will be conversationally laborious. Small talk at dinner parties is a rather torturous experience for the Analyst.

Analyst – career skills

The work environment is daily becoming more process-driven, whereby technology takes over the role of people. This development means there will be a growth in technology-related roles and it is important that you keep up to date with new emerging processes. You should continually look for courses or roles that will not just match but positively challenge and enhance your skills.

The dominant role of the Analyst is to offer a specialist technical skill to their employer, whereby soft skills are a secondary consideration. Your expertise is in what you know and your ability to apply your knowledge. A heart surgeon, a mathematical modeller, a jumbo jet pilot and a software engineer are employed predominantly for their technical expertise, and not for their amazingly friendly disposition or tacitness. These behaviours are less consequential. Clinically, scan the job boards for roles capitalising on your technical abilities. You should avoid roles with a high content of people dependent interaction such as sales or training. Analysts do not enjoy pressure selling and do not have the patience to be successful instructors. When the role has a people persuasive element or your work is supportive of sales presentations, you will have to be careful that you are not drawn into a sales type role that will not suit your personality. A salary where a large component is bonus or commission may be an indication that there is an obligation to perform and achieve, i.e. to sell. Avoid these advertisements.

The Analyst enjoys getting involved in technical work. You should therefore search for roles that will capitalise on your aptitude for engaging with complicated data, technical or scientific-based issues. The Analyst has strong management skills where projects involve a high degree of analysis and problem solving.

As an Analyst, you may have a tendency to understate your abilities and be over cautious in the roles for which you apply. Remember, new technologies are new to all candidates and you will have the aptitude and propensity to absorb new developments – be ambitious in your applications.

The Creative type is overlooked

You should know that the particular grouping of personality types is the result of my personal research. The inclusion of the Creative as a prominent type is unusual.

I believe that the Creative type is not given the prominence it requires within traditional personality analysis and categorisation. When I am coaching or recruiting Art Directors or other Executives requiring unique creative skills for the role, the candidates demonstrate clear characteristics that endorse their artistic and design talents not found in other personality types. When you think of art in terms of music, theatre, painting and sculpture, and when you realise that our physical environment is the result of purposeful architectural designs (not forgetting products, i.e. cars, mobiles, computers, etc.), creative design will have influenced the appearance and functional use in our day-to-day life.

Museums and art galleries in major cities throughout the world exhibit works of art that are a perpetual endorsement of creative talent: Picasso, Turner, Leonardo da Vinci, Monet, Bacon, Rothko; the list is extensive. Famous orchestras perform music – renditions of artists revered for their unique talents. Creative talent is demonstrated by so many job disciplines including architects, product designers, playwrights, songwriters, copywriters and authors, etc.

The thought processes of Creatives are highly individual and I have described their personality type through the identification of their unique traits. I believe that there are defining behaviours which are highly individualistic, separate and unique only to the Creative and, therefore, justify a standalone status.

You are not born a leader

A further deviation from common personality type grouping is not to nominate a director/leader as a distinct category. I agree with the American President, Barack Obama, when he stated in his inaugural speech, 'Power grows through its prudent use.' A director or leader is often categorised as a personality type. My experience leads me to form the view that a director or leader is a description of behaviour that is not innate but transient and reactive to situations. The leader profile is sometimes confused with aggressive or bullying behaviours, which are influenced by emotions and not personality traits.

All four types I have categorised can adopt a management and leadership style behaviour if required for their role. The Analyst may be a non-active participant at meetings, yet when they are chairing a meeting, they are highly structured and proactive. Behavioural adaptation is common in all types.

For example, many architectural practices will be successfully managed and directed by the Creative type. A Hospital Trust may be managed by a Supporter. Entrepreneurs will frequently fit the Influencer personality. Research and pharmaceutical organisations may be managed by the Analyst type.

The change of work culture from people to task, emphasised in the introduction, has also had an impact on management styles. The stereotypical perception of the corporate leader as a dominant 'follow me' extrovert with an amazing 'can do' attitude to all problems is now outdated.

The Analyst type now commonly manages corporations in today's climate where the understanding and application of technology and the formulation of sophisticated strategy is critical. This observation endorses my previous contention that leadership is not a personality trait, but an acquired or adopted skill to suit a situation. All four personality types are potential leaders.

The emerging nations have dramatically influenced the work environment. The commercial culture has had to adopt a fast-forward mentality. The life cycle of many products from design and development to production has been dramatically reduced. Companies are competing more on a world stage and globalisation has almost become a cliché. Technology has facilitated this change and we take for granted the fact that we can buy an airline or railway ticket without human interaction. Process drives organisations and employees follow the processes. Employee to employee interaction is reduced and many tiers of decision making are being performed and superseded by computers capable of processing data and presenting it in coherent conclusive report form.

The emerging nations have stimulated the outsourcing and off-shoring markets and the growth of computer technology and telecoms has facilitated a short-term 'now' culture, where the task rather than the people is the dominant focus.

This change in the commercial climate has an influence on the application of personality profiles. It means, for example, that the Analyst can be a successful entrepreneur, using the internet to market their products on a world stage. Historically, they would have been dependent on the Influencer to sell their products and services.

Now I know my personality

Chapters 2–3 of *Your Lowe Profile* will help you to identify your ideal role, coach you on writing a CV and making a job application, and Your Interview Profiler will give you an exciting format to win at interviews. Chapter 4, on doing the job, will coach you on how to interact more effectively at meetings and how to ensure that you are fulfilling your job role successfully.

Your Lowe Profile will include all the aspects and milestones of the various stages of your career. You can refer to the book selectively as events arise: a job application, an interview or meeting arranged at short notice, or a difficult situation at work.

The emphasis on knowing the real you, your strengths and how to apply them will ensure that you develop the optimum skill set to cope with and manage stressful challenges caused by today's fluid and demanding market. The incessant drive for growth and profit in an increasingly competitive global arena means that employers need to be strategically focused and performance orientated.

Chapter 2 Your Job Profile

The market today

Building your job profile is much aligned to, and influenced by, the condition of the job market. If there is a recession and an oversupply of your particular skills, then these factors will dictate your approach to your job search, which will require a flexible and creative attitude.

We can confidently describe the commercial climate as permanently evolving, competitive and uncertain of its own future. Our approach to job hunting must reflect this culture. Recognising these employment market dynamics will mean you will benefit positively from the skills coaching outlined in *Your Lowe Profile*.

Building your job profile

Your work experiences, your personal circumstances, your personal preferences and your personal development are never static. They are continually evolving and changing and your career goals and aspirations must reflect this change and adaptation.

If, by using a structured method, you can confidently define your ideal job profile incorporating your core skills, then this knowledge will help you to be more creative in your job search. You will confidently identify roles where, through skills transference, you can make a strong positive application. From my experience, many candidates are too insular in their job search and application of skills. There can be a tendency to underestimate their abilities, for example, not to apply for a particular role within an oil company as they have no previous experience of the industry.

Yet, frequently, employers do not require industry experience as the skills required are not industry specific. The purpose of this exercise, which invites you to define and review all the facets of a job profile, is to give you a stronger focus in terms of the roles you can target in your job search. To build a job profile you should incorporate the following five important elements, which, from research based on my interviewing experience, are considered to be critical to career choice:

1 Personal preferences.

2 Personal circumstances.

3 Soft skills.

4 Personal experience.

5 Remuneration.

Using these parameters, you can build your job profile and use it for job applications and as a reference for generating a professional CV. Review your choices and transfer your conclusion and comments to create Your Job Profiler. Be mindful that this exercise is a process, a road of discovery, not a sudden revelation. Let's look at the first signpost.

Part 1 Personal preferences

We all have individual dos and don'ts. Our choices are personal; they are not right or wrong and do not require justification or qualification. Reviewing your preferences helps you to focus on roles that fit your profile and eliminate those that clash with your selection criteria. Most candidates will consider the following options on a 'must have', 'must avoid' or 'don't mind' basis.

Location

Many people will choose to work and live in the same area. They feel part of and engage with their community. Others will travel out of the area to work and may feel that they neither have the time nor the inclination to integrate with the local community.

- Do you prefer a rural location where you can drive to work, or do you prefer to work in a large commercial conurbation?
- How important are the work and home locations to you?
- Do you feel strongly about either choice?

Hours

Employers will normally have a culture of nine to five, or long hours incorporating indefinite finishing times – which is your preference?

'Work is my life – I love it!'

'I am a member of a canoe club and I enjoy the twice weekly practice sessions.'

'It is important that I spend quality time with my family during the week as well as at weekends. Work/life balance is my priority.'

'I don't have time for hobbies – we are too busy at work.'

People/task environment

These comparisons will be familiar to you from when you were introduced in Chapter 1 to the various personality types. Follow the advice. If you are an Influencer or Supporter, your preference will be for roles that have a high level of people interaction. If you are an Analyst or Creative, the focus on the role content will be your choice. The job description will highlight the required skills and you can ascertain if they match your dominant personality traits.

Employer

The larger organisation will have good sports and social facilities and can offer a more structured career path. The smaller organisation can offer better scope for initiative, greater opportunity to feel part of a team and provides an environment whereby you can make an identifiable contribution.

- Do you prefer the work environment to be within central or local government, not for profit, a charity or a commercial organisation?

- Is it important for your employer to be nationally or internationally based? Do you prefer a large corporate environment or a small, more intimate working atmosphere?

- Do you prefer your employer to be a long-established organisation or a new start-up?

- Is ethical trading important to you in terms of product or service? Do you need to know your employer's sustainability policy if they have one?

Travel

This preference links well with the Location and Hours sections discussed earlier, but it is worth reviewing on a standalone basis. I know candidates who will only travel to work by car and who will not consider roles based in city centres due to the expense of parking and the inevitable travel congestion.

Where living environment is important, candidates may choose a seaside location and travel up to two hours to work. The possibility of lazy barbecuing on the beach on a balmy summer's evening keeps them going through the dark, cold, train-delayed winter commutes. If you are flexible regarding location, then securing the role first and then matching your other criteria can be a sensible approach to location.

Working from home for most or part of the week will become a more frequent phenomenon and you should factor this in to your choice of job and accommodation location. Working from home gives you the flexibility of living further from work as the long journey is a more occasional occurrence.

Hot-desking – attending the office only for client or internal staff meetings – can significantly reduce employers' accommodation overheads and is more likely to increase rather than diminish however much emphasis is put on the importance of face-to-face interaction.

In the hierarchy of choice, I would advise candidates to give primary consideration to their choice of location. Volatile recruitment markets mean your work location will change many times.

I have asked our Technical Director to comment on the influence of technology and how it impacts on the *modus operandi* of working behaviours:

The widespread availability of good internet connectivity and VPN technology means staff have access to the same applications whether they are working in or out of the office. 3G and wireless access in towns and cities means people can also continue to work whilst travelling or at a client site. Email on small hand-held devices gives people the ability to monitor their company mailbox continuously without sitting at a desk, and the work style of clocking on and clocking off is now becoming less common. This is particularly relevant when others with whom you are working are in a different time zone.

Use of instant messaging software is becoming more acceptable in organisations. As a communication tool, it can be more responsive than email. People use a telephone far less than they used to and they will often send an email instead. Instant messaging fits between telephony and email. Most instant messaging tools allow a user, once logged in, to set their availability status, which for example, may be 'busy', 'away' or 'online'. This provides the other user with some instant feedback and they can decide to send either an instant message or use another method of communication. It is used to get a quick answer.

Virtual meeting software further facilities collaborative working, allowing individuals to schedule meetings and send invites. Attendees use a link to log into a web page and they are presented with a dashboard view. Here they can see a list of others who have also joined. The meeting organiser is able to share a view of their desktop which the attendees can see on the main part of the dashboard screen. This may be a slideshow that they will use to present the meeting or it can be anything on their screen which they wish to discuss. If the attendees are using a headset, they can also talk to each other within the virtual meeting room using voice over IP protocol, which eliminates the need to setup a parallel conference call via the regular telephony system.

This type of virtual meeting software reduces even further the need to meet face to face, and a group of people working on the same project will be able to join the meeting from any location, if they have a good connection to the internet.

When the objective of a meeting is to sell or market a product or service, then most often the parties will meet face to face. The personal touch is regarded as critical to the sales process.

Summary questions:

Part 1 Personal preferences

What are your choice areas of work?

London City or West End.

How far in distance and time are you prepared to travel, and what are the costs?

Max 45 mins each way, maximum cost £100 per month.

Are you prepared to work weekends?

I will consider working weekends if I get paid overtime or additional time off in lieu.

What are your chosen hours of work?

Monday - Friday 9am - 5.30pm with 1 hour lunch.
Will welcome flexitime.

Are you prepared to be away from home on business – how often – how long?

Cannot travel at short notice for long periods due to personal commitments. Will consider travel if well planned in advance.

Are there extra curricular activities that you would sacrifice for work or would like to continue, for example, sport, hobbies, social groups or charity work?

Family commitments non-negotiable, could cut down on my social time and limit seeing friends to the weekend.

Additional notes:

Would be good if I could work every other Friday from home to be able to look after the kids whilst my partner is working at charity event.

Part 2 Personal circumstances

It is important to be realistic and confront factors that will limit your search options. All candidates have individual and particular dos and don'ts, and you should not view these restrictions negatively. They are just particular to you. Personal circumstances limit your choice when searching for suitable roles.

- You may dislike a certain mode of travel.
- You cannot cope with the rush-hour crush.
- You have a relative whom you need to care for.
- You are divorced and consider it important to live near to your children who are living with your ex-partner.
- You were born in a particular area and do not want to move despite the scarcity of employment opportunities.
- You have a large mortgage, are paying school fees and need a minimum salary of £100k. Work content and challenge may then be secondary considerations to salary level.

What are your family commitments? | Part 2 Personal circumstances

My daughter loves horse-riding. We take her twice a week.

What are your financial commitments?

Large mortgage, horse-riding fees and high community expenses.

Are many jobs available in your area?

Not locally but I'm prepared to make a long commute so that my family can benefit from local facilities.

Parts 3 and 4 Soft skills and personal experience

We have reviewed your preferences and circumstances and now we shall look at skills and experience. We could say that the first two are what you want and the latter two are what the job requires.

Overarching all of these is salary – the financial element. This will be dealt with in Part 5 Remuneration on page 49.

You will have already identified, and be familiar with, your personality strengths that are frequently referred to as soft skills, or the personal specification or attributes within a job description that may describe the need for the candidate to be flexible, creative, industrious, ambitious, to be able to multi-task and cope under pressure, etc.

Your particular skills will match your preference for a predominantly people or task environment, which you have previously reviewed in Chapter 1. However, soft skills cannot be considered on a standalone basis. Your skills are facilitators in the application of your other range of talents – your technical expertise. Though we can refer to soft skills and technical skills as separate, they are interdependent.

Technical skills are quantifiable and can be readily matched to advertisements as you scan the job boards. Technical skills will be obtained through education and work experience. The final parameter in building Your Job Profiler is to examine the extent and time over which you have acquired these skills.

When recruiting, the advertisements I write will frequently specify, 'You should have at least 5 years experience' or 'Ideally you will have 2 years experience' and salary levels will directly reflect the experience required.

This section on your job profile has been a prompt to encourage you to look more intently at your job opportunities and to apply a more selective mentality to the exercise.

Examples:

Soft skills — Part 3 Soft skills

I believe I have good communication skills and have given many internal presentations to groups of 20 staff. I frequently manage conference calls on highly technical IT issues and have recently completed my MBA, which I consider to be an endorsement of my ambition and determination towards self-development.

Soft skills: communication, analytical and ambitious

Personal experience — Part 4 Personal experience

I believe my History degree indicates my ability to decipher literary commentary and my two years experience as an Editorial Consultant for a leading magazine demonstrates my ability to choose topical subjects and to understand and apply my publishing expertise of copy writing, print production, marketing and distribution.

Technical skills: literacy, journalism, production, publishing, marketing and distribution.
Experience: literary training 3 years, publishing experience 2 years.

Part 5 Remuneration

By reading advertisements you will, through live research, get a good idea of salary ranges. Salaries are a personal subject and will be determined by your job priorities and domestic commitments. If job content and challenge are your most important criteria, then you will compromise on salary. There is no right or wrong. Some roles require a flexible attitude as the income initially may be below your expectation, but after six months or a year it may increase dramatically, subject to your performance. I have recently interviewed a financial analyst specialising in Mergers and Acquisitions who is prepared to accept a 50 per cent salary reduction. His current role demands that he works 15 hours per day and many weekends. Work/life balance is his motivation.

Location can be a major determinant regarding salaries. Inner-city roles will normally carry a higher salary than a country or suburban location. The compensation takes into account the travel inconvenience and cost, as well as supply and demand.

Salaries can only really be determined on an individual basis. The determinants are many and diverse and, therefore, throughout your working life, will require an adaptable and flexible approach, particularly during recessions and credit crunches. For instance, oil, pharmaceutical, finance, IT and consultancy have a reputation generally of being better paid than hotel and catering, whilst advertising, PR and design can be company dependent.

Salary packages will vary from employer to employer in terms of benefits. The range of benefits may include: basic annual salary and a commission or bonus (individual or company performance related), pension, which may or may not require an employee contribution (contributory/non-contributory), annual paid holiday, gym membership, maternity/paternity pay, private medical insurance, life assurance, company car or car allowance, flexible working hours, and share option schemes.

When reviewing vacancies, calculate your minimum salary in terms of your financial commitments, incorporating special factors such as commuting costs and, if relevant, accommodation. Be transparent about your salary expectations and if it is not specified in the advert, ask for clarification of the salary range. 'Should I discuss salary on interview?' 'Should I leave it until the second interview?' 'Will I appear too pushy or mercenary if I mention salary – they might think I am only interested in the money?' My advice is yes, do ask for clarification – it is not construed as a weakness, quite the reverse. 'I understand the salary range is...' 'I am seeking a minimum salary of...' are construed as non-aggressive formats to introduce the issue of remuneration. Headhunters will often play an important role in the negotiation of final terms.

Salary negotiation can provoke fascinating and diverse reactions. Some candidates will view a salary very personally: 'I am certainly not accepting that offer – it is far too low – I am worth a lot more.' This personal affront response will be the likely domain of the Supporter and the Influencer, whilst the Creative and the Analyst will be pragmatic and look elsewhere for the more competitive income.

The fluidity of the employment market requires greater flexibility on the candidate's part whereby employment on a temporary/contract basis has increased dramatically. More frequently, salary negotiation involves agreeing an hourly or daily rate. Where a technical skill is the dominant prerequisite for the role, there is a higher incidence of candidates working on a non-permanent basis. Examples are Creatives being employed as freelancers and IT specialists working on a contract basis.

View all salary negotiations on a supply/demand non-personal basis and you will most likely achieve a fair and realistic conclusion for both parties.

Part 5 Remuneration

What is your current salary?

£58,000 basic + free medical insurance and 10% bonus part personal and part company performance related.

What is your minimum requirement?

£55,000

What is the maximum salary of similar jobs? Will you receive benefits such as health insurance?

£45,000. Most employers do not offer free medical insurance or company pension.

Your Job Profiler

Part 1 Personal preferences — Location ✓ Hours ✓ Employer ✓ Travel ✓

Location: city, hours: 8-10 per day, employer: ideally corporate multinational, travel: public transport, journey time: max 45 mins, cost: max £100 per month

Part 2 Personal circumstances — Family ✓ Location ✓ Financial ✓

Family: married, 2 children, mother in care, location: cannot relocate, financial commitments: mortgage, children, school, carer, household

Part 3 Soft skills — Soft skills ✓

I believe I have good communication skills and have given many internal presentations to groups of 20 staff. I frequently manage conference calls on highly technical IT issues and have recently completed my MBA which I consider to be an endorsement of my ambition and determination towards self-development.

Part 4 Personal experience — Technical skills ✓ Experience ✓

I believe my History degree indicates my ability to decipher literary commentary and my two years experience as an editorial consultant for a leading magazine demonstrates my ability to choose topical subjects and to understand and apply my publishing expertise of copy writing, print production, marketing and distribution.

Part 5 Remuneration — Min requirement ✓ Ideal salary ✓ Benefits ✓

Min 50k to cover monthly commitments (cannot go under); ideal 65k (10k more than current role); must have health insurance, pension fund and lifecover - profit share would be considered

The benefits of building your job profile

The benefits you have accrued from defining and building your job profile are:

- more focused search, whereby you only target roles that match your criteria
- less time wasting, whereby you may historically have made aspirant applications and 'hoped for the best'
- higher ratio of applications to interview
- higher ratio of interviews to job offers
- objective achieved.

You have identified your personality type and your strengths, and you have applied this knowledge to building your job profile. This means you can now capitalise on this knowledge and move to the most exciting stage – applying for the job. You can use this information to write a successful CV.

Writing a successful CV

Think content

How to construct a good CV is one of the most written about subjects in the area of career advice and coaching.

It is difficult for the reader to know what is correct advice. Clearly, the collective advice given cannot all be correct, as many of the books and articles on the subject contradict themselves. I shall introduce you to what I consider to be the ideal format from the employer's perspective. However, before I do, let's look at some common perceptions and misconceptions. This will encourage you to explore the real role of this summary description of yourself (Curriculum Vitae).

An analogy that candidates have found useful is to compare looking for a job with the search for a new car.

When you plan to purchase a second-hand car, you will have prequalified certain details and preferences: age, manufacturer, model, mileage, price range, colour, service history, condition, number of owners, and location for convenient viewing. The following advertisement will probably not create much enthusiasm.

> **Advertisement**
>
> Clean, well-maintained Ford Focus with low mileage. Reliable and regularly serviced. Must sell as owner is relocating abroad. Very competitive price and offers accepted.

On the other hand, you may contact this owner for an exploratory conversation if it fits your criteria of price, etc:

> **Advertisement**
>
> Ford Focus ('06 model) Silver. One owner from new. Full service history. 18,000 miles. Showroom condition £6,000 ono. Oxford, city location…

These comparisons, though exaggerated, make a salient point regarding the structure of your CV and why you must emphasise detail at all times. The pervading theme is to know that the reader is seeking factual information – not hyped generalisations.

Think context

I review many CVs with introductory mission statements:

'A highly successful executive with a track record of achievement and excellent communication skills now seeking a challenging role to capitalise on a broad range of proven skills.'

I do not give consideration to these statements – they give me no qualitative information. I need detail and facts and all statements must be contextually placed. Follow my CV format so that recruiters can make a fair assessment based on your real performance, not generalised, hyped narrative. Your CV will stand out from the crowd for its clarity, its ease of legibility, creating a positive attitude in the reader's mind.

You are, in fact, facilitating the recruiter to make a real and fair assessment of how well you match the vacancy – which will be composed of a factual, not hyped, description of duties and responsibilities. Discussions that will ring a familiar note:

'How long should a CV be?'

'How many pages?'

'Should I write a mission statement?'

'People keep telling me to mention my achievements, but I can't really think of any big achievements – I just did the job!'

'Sell yourself – but I am not a sales person…'

'Be brief. The reader does not have much time! CVs are scanned first, not read in detail. But what does "not much time" mean – 1 minute, 20 minutes?'

'Put all your details on one page – if they require more information, they will ask you for it. But my present CV is three pages – which bits do I take out?'

'Use bullet points!'

'Mention your hobbies so that the reader will have a better understanding of the real you!'

My advice is, without apology, directive and based on over 30 years experience of reading CVs and interviewing candidates for real live current vacancies and, because I am at the sharp end, I know at first hand what works and what does not. My experience spans all industries and services and includes some of the world's most prestigious recruitment projects. Each day I may review up to 100 CVs and I can pass on that experience to you to ensure that yours is in the selected category.

I have used this format when coaching main Board Directors of large corporations and when lecturing MBA students at leading universities from all world continents. The format is structured as a template that can embrace all skills of all employees from all industries including all nationalities.

So let us talk about CV writing and its format. Once compiled, it can be used for all applications. You do not have to generate a new CV for each job. The objective of the CV is to secure an interview for a suitable role, and I deliberately use the word 'suitable'. Its objective is not to overstate or distort your experience to gain an interview for a role in which you are neither interested nor competent to fulfil.

Think audience

Let us look at the situation from the recruiter's point of view. One of your staff has just handed in their notice and you need to replace them quickly. Or you have had a meeting with your colleagues and you have decided that, due to business expansion, you need to recruit a new person. You spend some time drawing up a job description.

The job description will list the soft skills and technical skills required to carry out the role. Soft skills mean personality characteristics, for example determined, communicative, analytical, etc. Technical skills mean the candidate's ability and expertise in performing technical tasks, for example IT, accounting and marketing.

If your skills, as specified in your CV and in particular your technical skills, match the job requirement and your application is supported with an articulate email, then you will have an excellent chance of being called for an interview.

A further scenario: Imagine you are a company director who is seeking a candidate with two years experience of Apple Mac graphics packages to run and manage your design studio. The ideal candidate will have a media or design-related degree. You receive an email from a candidate with four years Mac experience who has supervised a competitor's studio, has a degree in Product Design and lives five miles from your company's offices. You immediately respond to the candidate and invite them for an interview. The candidate applied at the right time and the details of their CV were clear. The recruiter was able to establish that there was a good match between their requirements and this candidate's skills.

If the next email you receive is from an accountant sent out speculatively, you will have no time to read it as you do not have a vacancy for an accountant. If, however, the next email is from another studio manager, I am sure you would read it avidly.

Exactly the same criterion applies to scanning a CV. I will only spend time on those CVs that match my job descriptions and, like the studio manager example, which I identify as a good match.

This means that 'mission statements' are irrelevant as they do not comply with the role for which you have sent your CV. Frequently, I have read mission statements, 'My career goal is to join a large multinational…' when the CV sent is in support of a role where the client employs 100 staff and is UK based! They can be read as being too non-relational and making exaggerated claims: 'Highly successful executive with a consistent track record of achievement and strong people management skills.' When I am reading a CV, I want facts that I can compare with a job description. 'Consistent track record' – doing what? 'People management skills' – how many and when?

Supportive statements can be included in your accompanying email where, from our examples, you can recognise how powerful and influential good contextual narrative can be in securing the interviews. Remember, I read CVs from a positive disposition and I am hoping that your CV matches the job profile – a fact that explodes the 'time' myth. You will read advice that employers will only have a few minutes to read your CV – that you will need something that will catch and hold their attention so you will have to sell yourself and produce a big mission statement or profile. Hopefully, I have discounted these claims – a CV is primarily a factual information document, a summation of your experience to be compared with a job description.

The description should be clear, legible and factual. A CV then is a transparent, easily legible description of you and your experience presented in a positive and complimentary format.

This means your CV is:

- easy to read – logical/transparent
- descriptive/informative – containing your personal and employment details
- an account of your achievements and successes, always in a contextual format. What organisation did you work for, what did they do and when? Give details.

A CV works if it explains your personal details, education and work experience clearly, and if the recruiter has a vacancy that matches your skills.

A CV is always a contextual document. On its own, it serves no purpose.

This point is important as much of the opinion concerned with CV writing is personally dovetailed as though the candidate were commissioning a painting or portrait of themselves. Try, then, to focus on the functional rather than the personal perspective of CV writing. Adopt the simple uncomplicated template as outlined on the following page. Remember, a CV is an easy-to-read description about yourself. It is, in fact, common sense.

CV composition

A professional CV comprises two sections: a **main section** and a **supportive section**.

Part 1 Main section — Personal details, education, employment history

Personal details

Name:
Address:

Home telephone:
Mobile:
Email address:
Nationality:

Education

University/college:
Location:
Dates: from/to:
Qualifications:

School/college:
Location:
Dates: from/to:
Qualifications:

Employment history

Name of most recent employer:
Location:
Website:
Dates:
Description of employer:
Job title:
Duties and responsibilities:

Start with your most recent employer and use this format for each one. Adding a brief description of your employer will contextually place all further details about you in terms of your performance and responsibilities. Certain roles may require previous industry-specific experience and it is important that the recruiter can identify the match. A short descriptive paragraph of your previous employers, their size in terms of turnover, number employed, product or service description and your particular division, role and its activities, if relevant, is helpful to the reader.

Comment on how well you succeeded in carrying out your duties and responsibilities. Your comments should be well grounded, not exaggerated.

Part 2 Support section
Projects, technical skills, additional information

Addendum of projects

Client:
Description:
Your role:

This section is optional and will only apply where your work was primarily project, task specific or assignment based and you wish to have the opportunity to be more elaborate by describing a sample of your main projects.

The dynamic change in today's working environment means it is more segmented with less of a continuum component resulting in duties and responsibilities being more project orientated.

Technical skills

IT skills:
Language skills:

List your IT and/or language skills which you have developed and were core to your success at work.

Additional information

Hobbies:
Interests:

This is a general 'catch all' section where you can itemise professional memberships, awards, prizes, achievements, courses, hobbies or interests which you consider to be important either on a personal basis or as a skill endorsement.

Your CV template

Part 1 Main section

Personal details

David Rogers	Home telephone:	020 974 4298
70 Chalkson Street	Mobile:	09676 412 981
London BR6 978	Email address:	e-mail@domain.com
	Nationality:	British

Education

London University
Regent Street, London
1999–2002
BA History 2:1

Ronan College
Mulberry Street, London
1992–1999
3 A levels (History, Geography, Biology)
9 O levels

Employment history

Barchester & Royce Ltd
Castle Street, Edinburgh
www.barchesterandroyce.com

June 2007 to present

Barchester & Royce Ltd is a prestigious international group of management consultants. They concentrate on actively partnering large multinational corporates to formulate their global strategy. They employ approximately 6,000 consultants and have a turnover of £450m.

Marketing Manager

I manage a department of 10 staff and have overall responsibility for the £2m budget.
I promote our brand using all the current social network media and I am tasked with managing all channels of online marketing, in particular SEO and SEM. I am responsible for the events team, which organises conferences, seminars, breakfast meetings and industry events to promote our brand and create new business. The Board is keen that we identify new emerging markets with expansion potential.

My role is key as it is the link between the consultants and external stakeholders including clients, PR agencies and the mainstream media.

I ensure that our corporate policy is compliant with best sustainability practice and I have embedded these practices in our corporate mission statement and marketing campaigns.

My role requires a wide range of skills and has a direct and positive impact in generating new revenue. Innovation and embracing new technology is my forte and the Board has acknowledged my key contribution through the 30% increase in my annual budget.

CV continued...

Backbone Ltd
Marshall Street, London
www.backboneltd.com

Sept 2002 to May 2007

Backbone Ltd is a small niche market research agency which helps its clients to stay ahead of their competition through quality research. The company employs 30 staff and has an £18m turnover.

Marketing Executive

My main responsibility was working as a research analyst on behalf of a broad portfolio of clients. My main activities included consulting, law, accounting, oil, construction and manufacturing.

I applied various quantitative and qualitative analytical techniques to their competitiveness, the corporate identity and the development of marketing strategy.

I personally presented actionable recommendations to our clients and was responsible for our 10 main accounts, which generated an annual revenue of £7m (for an example, see addendum section below).

Part 2 Support section

Addendum of projects

UK leisurewear market

Large adult clotheswear retailer with 150 branches in the UK

Budget: £400,000

Our client previously specialised in business wear for the 25–40 year age group. They wished to expand their business into other market segments beginning with youth leisurewear.

Using competitor data and observing the trends from the particular niche market leaders and having conducted a product portfolio analysis, I commissioned two designers, who were at the cutting edge of British fashion, to produce samples for an exclusive trendy range which was bold in style and priced at the middle of the market.

I presented my recommendations to the Board incorporating strongly supported gap analysis and reports which were the outcome of comprehensive and complex qualitative and quantitative analysis. The Board accepted my recommendations and the initial launch was very successful and exceeded its target share by 40%. The client has commissioned a further project with a budget of £600,000 to determine the best strategy to enter the adult market with a similar product range.

Technical skills

IT skills: Excel, PowerPoint, Adobe Illustrator
Language skills: French (conversational)

Additional information

CIM (obtained 2007)
Currently studying for an MBA

This format is logical and gives you an excellent platform to market yourself. Use it for all situations. It is the critical component for the next important section 'Finding the job' (see page 63).

In Summary

Use a narrative format

The most effective CVs use a narrative format describing the work content and the candidate's involvement. This style is persuasive and has a positive influence on the recruiter. This transparency of content and the fluency of construction represent a successful and articulate candidate.

Commonly, candidates are advised to use bullet points for sentence construction and to ensure that the CV is no longer than two pages. This advice may sound good, but has no rational or authoritative foundation. I feel my reading skills are advanced enough to understand the significance of each word or sentence without it being highlighted by a repetitive bullet point. Don't use bullet points; use full descriptive sentences telling your positive story. This narrative format gives you the opportunity for more intelligent composition and chronological descriptions.

Two pages or longer?

The 'two pages' opinion also indicates a misunderstanding of the focus of the CV. If I were a Managing Director, I don't think the selection panel would be over impressed with my two-page crammer. Clearly, the number of pages will be determined by your seniority and years of experience. It is read for its content, not its length.

If you are a consultant or architect where the nature of your technical expertise is determined by the nature of the projects you performed, which may include a variety of assignments, then you should list a sample of the projects separately, detailing their content, purpose and your role.

Similarly, IT executives will list their experience of applications, programming languages and hardware. Creative candidates with graphic design expertise should have a portfolio that supports their technical experience required for the role. The various projects, their content and your involvement can be separately listed under the title 'Addendum of projects'. This allows the recruiter to refer to the information if they consider it relevant and does not make the CV appear too elongated.

Finding the job

Register with online services

Technology continues to facilitate the exercise of searching for those interesting matching roles and this is the most common and effective method for securing employment in the present market. Interrogating job boards is now a straightforward exercise, just requiring patience and an attitude of thoroughness. Some sites will capture all job advertising, including newspapers, consultants, boards, magazines and employers. Through frequent interrogation, you will become familiar with the sites that are most relevant to you. Again, I emphasise being selective and using only my recommended qualitative method of application.

It is easy to identify and search the major websites, job boards and the specialist sites. Be mindful, however, to make purposeful applications when you have identified jobs in which you are particularly interested and which suit your range of skills. Refer to the section 'Responding to job advertisements' on page 65, and closely follow the advice. Do not send your CV speculatively and do not send your CV without an accompanying email.

'Please find enclosed my CV for the position of… If you need any further information, please contact me.'

This type of application normally results in employers reaching for the delete key. It is not a serious application. In my role, I write and place advertisements on the main job boards. I then review the hundreds of replies and call about five per cent for interview. Knowing what works, I can give you that 'inside track' expertise to dramatically increase your chances of being in that five per cent.

Apply direct

Use the internet to identify organisations that you consider may benefit from your skills. The current vacancies will normally be listed on their website. In the section 'Responding to job advertisements', I shall elaborate on the most effective method and approach to use. Send your CV together with a strong email identifying and outlining four of your skills that you consider to be relevant to the organisation and its activities. Follow your application with a further telephone call or, if you prefer, email.

Network through your contacts

Today's market offers greater flexibility in choice of career structure and skills application. This flexibility creates an environment whereby the candidate can be more independent in their application of skills. This situation means that the candidate is less reliant on the 'who you know' phenomena and personal recommendations. It is, however, useful to network through friends and family by way of finding out background information about an organisation that they know as an employee or supplier.

Currently, the vast majority of candidates gain employment through the internet rather than personal contacts. The internet as a recruitment vehicle allows for more objectivity in your consideration of a role, rather than joining a company because a friend works there or recommended you and then two months later realising that the work does not really match your skills or career aspirations.

Job advertisements – in print

This is also an important source for identifying interesting vacancies. Use the national press, scanning both the display and semi-display advertisements. Use periodicals, magazines, and industry-specific or specialist publications. Familiarise yourself with the content and classification of recruitment advertising that is carried by these publications. You may be surprised, for example, in the UK, *The Grocer* carries a comprehensive range of advertisements for roles that are not necessarily compliant with its title.

The identification of market trends, salary ranges and employment growth areas is important information that you will gain from scanning these publications.

Recruitment consultants

This is an area you will have already covered through your applications on the leading websites. Many recruitment consultancies do not use their own websites, but place their advertisements on the job boards. Do not send your CV speculatively as recruitment consultants work on the basis of identifying an application against an intended vacancy. If you are lucky enough, they might occasionally approach you when you will be the subject of that ego-boosting headhunt. However, do not let emotional reaction cloud your judgement. Ask the headhunter why they have called you and what they know about your skills. You may be surprised and disappointed at their vacant answers and then realise that the call was a speculative canvassing exercise on their part.

The professional headhunter will do comprehensive research and only call you to discuss a serious career opportunity that fits your profile.

Responding to job advertisements

Never send a CV on its own – you must explain the reason and context in which you are sending it.

You may be sending it in response to an advertisement and you must accompany the CV with a well-constructed email (or letter) outlining your reason for applying for the role.

A well-written email, outlining your suitability, will dramatically increase your chance of being called for interview.

An advertisement is a summary of a job description and will mention the salient skills required. When reading the advertisement, firstly identify the critical compulsory skills and construct your accompanying email in a way that demonstrates your expertise in that area.

'I notice in your advertisement that you are seeking a candidate with analytical skills. In my current role, I research statistical reports and compile a summary...'

Job descriptions, which are the source of information for the advertisement, will vary in length and detail. Some will be extremely cursory and brief. In some cases, the recruiter will not have a written job description but will work from a verbal briefing. In other cases, there will be a detailed and comprehensive description of the role. Terminology will vary but typically will include the purpose of the job, the description of the organisation, competencies and levels, experience, knowledge, qualifications, duties, responsibilities, activities, soft skills, technical skills, location and remuneration package. The description will specify and demarcate between essential required skills and those that are desirable but not critical.

When you are applying for a particular role, identify four skills requirements from the advertisement that you think strongly match your profile. Outline your relevant experience or competencies that endorse your suitability for the role. Your email should be specific and concise. Occasionally, some advertisements will invite you also to telephone to ascertain your initiative, where good communication skills are critical to the role such as advertising, **PR**, business development and situations where you deliver client presentations. Make sure you do telephone. Use the content and format of your email as a guide for presenting yourself verbally.

Having submitted your application, you wait for a response. Don't expect an acknowledgement. Recruiters will not have the time to respond to each application and will contact only those candidates whom they would like to call for interview. They may contact you by telephone or, more frequently, by email. Your job search is influenced by many unforeseen factors. The number of responses I receive will vary between 10 and 200 per role. Therefore, if a recruiter does not invite you for interview, it may not be that you don't have the experience and competency to carry out the role successfully, but merely that another candidate fits the criteria more closely in terms of location and competitor experience.

In your skills profile and CV construction you have identified your dominant competencies and you should only apply to roles that match those. Be selective; only make quality applications. Don't scan the job boards and apply to roles that look vaguely interesting with no regard for competencies required. Don't just click and send with the inevitable one or two-liner.

'Please find enclosed my CV for the role of... If you require any further information, please email me or phone me on my mobile. I look forward to an early response.'

This type of click and send normally promotes a click and delete.

I review applications from a positive perspective. Recruiters are hoping to find a match. As I am continually reviewing job descriptions, writing advertisements and managing responses daily, I am familiar with the winning formula. Follow the recommendations on CV and email construction and you will increase your chances of being in that five per cent whom we are delighted to call for an interview.

Consider the following advertisements that I wrote and posted online on leading job boards when recruiting on behalf of prestigious clients. You can then view real responses at first hand. This exercise will demonstrate the importance of formulating quality applications and dramatically increase your ratio of positive replies.

> **Advertisement**
>
> ECONOMIST/ANALYST | WEST END | £80,000
>
> This is an exciting new role with a prestigious investment institution where you will be responsible for economic analysis, statistical reporting, competitor analysis, creating working groups, organising and speaking at seminars, etc.
>
> The variety and scope are the most appealing elements, as well as the intellectual challenge and the opportunity for creative thinking in terms of best strategy and trends.
>
> Ideally, you will have a degree in economics and a further five years experience in a similar role.
>
> Telephone me, John Lowe, direct on...

Four key attributes, therefore, that a suitable candidate for this Economist/Analyst role might possess include:

- excellent analytical skills
- flexibility
- strong interpersonal skills
- creativity.

We receive over 100 CVs with supporting emails everyday, some of which are replicated on the following pages. Judge which ones are the serious applications and the ones which we consider to be the just 'click and send'. Here are some examples from our inbox:

> **Email | To: John Lowe | Subject: Advert**
>
> Dear John,
>
> I am enclosing my CV for the online advertisement ref 61279428. I am going on holiday on Tuesday but can be contacted on my mobile even though I shall be in Cyprus.
>
> I am very interested in the job as I think it really suits me. So if you have any queries please call me even though I'm on holiday. I shall be back in the UK on Monday.
>
> Hope to hear from you.
>
> A. Sample

What job is this applicant responding to? The reference number is the online advertiser's, not our reference. The respondent does not demonstrate any commitment or engagement with the role. **Deleted**.

> **Email | To: John Lowe | Subject: Advert**
>
> Dear Sir/Madam,
>
> I wish to apply for the position of Analyst because I think that I would be a suitable candidate. For this reason, please find attached my CV. If there is anything else needed in order to consider me, please let me know. Once you have had a look at my CV, if you are interested, I would be happy to discuss what I am doing now and my future aspirations.
>
> Yours sincerely,
>
> A. Sample

This example sounds polite, but it **does not engage** with the role and its responsibilities and the applicant is responding in a 'click and send' manner.

> **Email | To: John Lowe | Subject: Advert**
>
> Dear John,
>
> I am responding to your ad published online for an analyst. I enclose a copy of my CV for your attention.
>
> I am currently working within the policy department of a prestigious merchant bank where I am supporting the department manager with economic and competitor analysis. I present my computations in the form of reports and, where the content is relevant, I take an active part in client seminars.
>
> I have a Maths degree and enjoy the aspects that your advertisement is emphasising, particularly the intellectual and the challenge of combining my creative and statistical skills.
>
> I shall look forward to hearing from you.
>
> Yours sincerely,
>
> A. Sample

Brief and to the point. An enthusiastic response – **I invited the candidate for interview**.

> **Email | To: John Lowe | Subject: Advert**
>
> Dear John,
>
> Please find enclosed my CV for the Economist job.
>
> Thanks,
>
> A. Sample

It is surprising how frequently I receive this type of response. **Deleted.**

Advertisement

DIRECTOR OF STRATEGY | RETAIL APPAREL or FMCG | LONDON

£75,000 + executive package

This is a challenging role in that it combines two critical skills – the ability to develop strategic plans and the ability to manage and implement the strategy.

The Director will be responsible for achieving volume targets for children's soft lines in the UK, which are marketed through licensees and retailers. You will be representing an organisation and brand that is a household name and carries a worldwide reputation for quality and innovation.

You will need excellent technical skills in consumer marketing, brand management, P&L, corporate business planning and strategy. The ideal candidate will have a first degree and an MBA, with top-level negotiating skills and the flexibility to combine entrepreneurial drive with corporate objective.

You may prefer to discuss this exciting role with our Consultant on… prior to making a formal application.

We again highlight the dominant skills required:

- Develop and implement strategic plans.
- Results orientated.
- Consumer marketing.
- Profit and loss.
- Negotiation.
- Initiative.

Your email should include at least four skills that endorse your suitability for the role and match those specified in the advertisement.

> **Email | To: John Lowe | Subject: Director of Strategy**
>
> Dear John,
>
> The role of Director of Strategy appeals to me as it replicates my current role as Director of Communications with a large multiple retailer. I am responsible for the formulation of our global strategy throughout Europe and China and I supervise a team of 5 who are responsible for implementing the plans. I carry Profit and Loss responsibility for £20 million for my department.
>
> I manage a sub division within my department, which is involved in brand and consumer marketing. I have a BSc in Biology and an MBA from London.
>
> I enclose my CV and look forward to hearing back from you.
>
> Yours sincerely,
>
> A. Sample

A strong, focused reply, which endorses a range of synergistic skills within brief, direct narrative. The candidate was enthusiastically **invited for interview**.

> **Email | To: John Lowe | Subject: Director of Strategy**
>
> Dear John,
>
> Please find enclosed my CV for the Director of Strategy. You will see from my CV that I have been involved in global strategic planning and marketing for the Auto industry for 5 years. Previously, I was manager of strategy for a building products organisation specialising in interior products.
>
> I feel I have the experience you are looking for and look forward to your call.
>
> Yours sincerely,
>
> A. Sample

Auto and interior products are technical experiences that do not match the job requirements. It would be better for the candidate to adopt a more selective approach at this level and seek roles that capitalise on their unique experiences. **Deleted**.

> **Email | To: John Lowe | Subject: Director of Strategy**
>
> Dear Mr Lowe,
>
> I would be grateful if you would let me know if my application is successful for the Director of Strategy job. I have an MBA and I am looking for an executive position.
>
> Yours sincerely,
>
> A. Sample

Not an engaging response. **Deleted**.

> **Email | To: John Lowe | Subject: Director of Strategy**
>
> Dear John,
>
> I am hoping to find the opportunity to telephone you later today and, in the meantime, I would like to endorse my interest in your role for Director of Strategy – Retail. I have worked for an international retailer for the last 5 years where I am responsible for branding, product selection, sales and distribution of our entire apparel range, of which 30% is children's fashion.
>
> My previous 4 years was with a major food retailer where I had total European P&L responsibility for all ready-meal products. My experience of apparel, the retail market and ultimately P&L fits your dominant criteria of technical skills and I shall look forward to the opportunity of talking with you to define the people specification.
>
> Yours sincerely,
>
> A. Sample

This is a strong response. The candidate has taken the time and care to engage with the advertisement. A positive reply – the candidate was **invited for interview**.

> **Advertisement**
>
> REGIONAL MANAGER SOUTH EAST | CONSTRUCTION EQUIPMENT
>
> £60,000 + base + Up to 30% bonus + executive car and benefits
>
> Leadership, initiative, teamwork, industry leading customer service, sound business strategy, profitable growth – these are the dominant factors that will be the hallmark of a successful Regional Manager.
>
> This prestigious and high-profile organisation has a national and worldwide reputation for innovation, product quality and reliability. The extensive range of equipment includes excavators, loaders, dozers, rollers, dumpers, telehandlers, compactors and the applications will cover construction, quarrying, waste, demolition and material handling.
>
> The Regional Manager's role could be described as the General Manager of the South East region as they will have the autonomy to apply their own skills in creative thinking, service delivery and leadership whilst being responsible for the P&L and all budgets.
>
> The ideal candidate will have a track record of successfully managing a team of 50 plus and the technical experience gained in a similar or related environment. If you are very ambitious and seeking that ultimate challenge which packages all the exciting ingredients of a world-class organisation, internationally known products, real career growth and dynamic management responsibilities, then telephone John Lowe in confidence on…

There is a wide range of experiences to choose from that are highlighted in this advertisement. Choose four.

- Leadership/management – 50 staff.
- Construction industry plant.
- Profit and loss.
- Business strategy.
- Customer focus.
- Performance orientated.
- Ambitious.

> **Email | To: John Lowe | Subject: Regional Manager Construction**
>
> Dear John,
>
> Further to our telephone conversation, I can confirm that I have 10 years experience within the mobile plant construction industry. I began my career as a Sales Executive and then joined the marketing department and, latterly, my role as a commercial manager incorporates P&L, recruitment and planning.
>
> Consistently since my sales role I have exceeded all targets by 10% and I am now seeking a new challenge as stated in your advertisement.
>
> I shall call you again on Tuesday to answer any questions you may have.
>
> Yours sincerely,
>
> A. Sample

This is a strong response and, though brief, reactive in terms of the advertisement's specification. The candidate was **invited for interview**.

> **Email | To: John Lowe | Subject: Regional Manager Construction**
>
> Dear John,
>
> I have been working in the construction industry for 25 years and know most of the major contractors. I have excellent management skills and in my present job I work under pressure whilst multi-tasking.
>
> Let me know if my application is successful.
>
> Yours sincerely,
>
> A. Sample

This response is majoring on the 'construction' industry experience and ignores the rest of the criteria. **Deleted**.

> **Advertisement**
>
> MANAGING DIRECTOR | EUROPE | MANAGEMENT CONSULTANCY
>
> £400,000 + executive package
>
> Our client is seeking an exceptional and insightful leader to manage new and exciting growth opportunities in the UK and Europe.
>
> The dynamic change and short-termism that is prevalent in today's corporate environment is causing an onerous challenge to executives in terms of future planning and shareholders' expectations.
>
> Our client advises medium to large international corporations on best strategic definition and implementation to manage and sustain performance improvement and growth. The Managing Director will have the support of a strong, competent Board, which is receptive to innovation and positive leadership. The ideal candidate will have exceptional skills in corporate management, strategic thinking, organisational planning and a successful track record of management within the service sector.
>
> Our client has 15 offices throughout Europe and employs 3,000 staff. To apply for this role send your CV to John Lowe or, if you wish to find out more information, call John in confidence on…

We can identify the following skills as critical from the tone of the advertisement:

- Leadership – 3,000 staff.
- International experience.
- Planning.
- Determining strategy.
- Service sector.
- Performance orientation.
- Innovative.

> **Email | To: John Lowe | Subject: Managing Director**
>
> Dear John,
>
> I am interested in applying for the Managing Director's role.
>
> I am currently the lead Consultant in a team of 500 where I am responsible for their performance and development. Our Consultancy is one of the world's leaders in global strategy and I am now seeking a new operational challenge where I can capitalise on my 15 years experience with my current organisation.
>
> Please let me know the recruitment process.
>
> Yours sincerely,
>
> A. Sample

A good response. The candidate may not be logistically senior enough for the role in terms of people numbers and international exposure; however, they are **worth inviting for interview** as a candidate 'with potential' rather than proven track record. Personality and interview performance will be critical here.

> **Email | To: John Lowe | Subject: Managing Director**
>
> Dear John,
>
> I am applying for the position of MD. I am working as a management consultant since being made redundant from my last job. I enjoy travel and in my present job I travel extensively. You will see from my CV that I have the relevant experience and am used to managing people. I am available immediately.
>
> Yours sincerely,
>
> A. Sample

This applicant does not engage with the critical content of the advertisement. Management consultants require good report writing skills and the respondent must therefore give a coherent account of themselves. **Deleted**.

> **Email | To: John Lowe | Subject: Managing Director**
>
> Dear John,
>
> I wish to formally apply for your MD role, Europe. Fifteen years ago I commenced my career with a leading management consultant where I ultimately managed a department specialising in organisational change and development.
>
> In my current role, I am the MD for a leading software house supplying technical integrated solutions to the publishing industry. My brief includes the UK and Europe.
>
> I am responsible for setting strategy, identifying new markets and product innovation and ultimately corporate performance which has grown 20% year on year under my stewardship. We employ 2,400 staff in 7 countries.
>
> I am interested in the role because of the new challenge it presents, capitalising on my management consulting expertise and combined with my successful track record of leading a prestigious organisation in a very competitive market. I enthusiastically wish to apply for the role and can be reached in confidence by email or on my direct number.
>
> Yours sincerely,
>
> A. Sample

A strong application endorsing the synergy of technical and soft skills and operational performance – the dominant criteria. The candidate was **invited for interview**.

> **Email | To: John Lowe | Subject: Managing Director**
>
> Dear John,
>
> I am interested in applying for the position of European Managing Director. Could you please forward me a job description and application form?
>
> Yours sincerely,
>
> A. Sample

No comment needed here. **Deleted.**

> **Advertisement**
>
> GRADUATE PUBLISHING | LONDON | £18,500
>
> This is an excellent opportunity for a graduate wishing to develop a career in publishing. Our client is a successful publisher of a range of magazines covering a wide subject area including Health, Auto, Music, Business, Property and Leisure.
>
> The successful candidate will spend time in various departments such as advertising, editorial, production, subscriptions and IT.
>
> The uniqueness of this role is the fact that the graduate will, after a year's introduction, have the opportunity to work in the department of their choice.
>
> Send your CV and an email outlining your reasons for applying to johnlowe@...

This is an interesting exercise in terms of identifying the required key skills. The advertisement does not nominate competencies, but rather describes an opportunity for potential publishing graduates. Therefore, we can be assumptive and address the following key issues:

- Why are you choosing a career in publishing?
- Ambitious – explain and elaborate.
- Excellent communication skills are foundational to publishing, therefore the content and construction of your email will be judged in that context.

> **Email | To: John Lowe | Subject: Graduate Publishing vacancy**
>
> Dear John,
>
> I am attaching my CV for the job you are advertising.
>
> Yours,
>
> A. Sample

Easy decision. **Deleted**.

> **Email | To: John Lowe | Subject: Graduate Publishing vacancy**
>
> Dear John,
>
> I have an honours degree in History from Durham and would like to apply for the Graduate role in publishing.
>
> I deliberately chose a literary subject and history in particular as, similar to publishing, it is conveying a message.
>
> I am an avid reader of a wide range of magazines and, in particular, Music and Health as they endorse my interests. I am a good mixer having established a wide range of friends at university and college and would enjoy the experience of interacting with the various departments.
>
> Publishing is my first career choice and I enclose my CV for your attention.
>
> Yours sincerely,
>
> A. Sample

Good reply. Took care and time to write. The candidate was **called for interview**.

> **Email | To: John Lowe | Subject: Graduate Publishing vacancy**
>
> Dear John,
>
> I enjoy writing and reading fiction. I enjoy current affairs and discussing topical events. Books are important in today's society when we watch so much television.
>
> Thank you for your time and I look forward to hearing from you.
>
> Best wishes,
>
> A. Sample

Content and quality is poor and there is no engagement with the advertisement. **Deleted**.

> **Email | To: John Lowe | Subject: Graduate Publishing vacancy**
>
> Dear John,
>
> I am particularly interested in your advertisement which offers a structured career in publishing. I have a degree in English and was the Editor of the University student magazine with a circulation of 20,000. I regularly attend my local gym, play the guitar to Grade 7 standard and am a member of the local hockey team. I occasionally 'dabble' in stocks and shares. My wide interests replicate the breadth of your publications.
>
> I can attend an interview at short notice.
>
> Yours sincerely,
>
> A. Sample

The response focuses exclusively on the role. The candidate was **called for interview**.

Recommendations:

- Only apply for roles that really interest you and which match your skills.

- Don't send your CV speculatively in the hope that 'something will come up'.

- When you have identified a suitable role, spend time analysing the key skills required and then describe how they match your particular profile.

Chapter 3 Your Interview Profile

This is an exciting subject to write about. The point of an interview is to get the job. A really good performance on interview will result in a job offer. Your whole life changes. You text friends, leave messages and send emails. You want to share the good news with everyone. It is amazing to think of the changes a new job brings to your lifestyle: new motivation, new journeys to make, new colleagues to meet, and a new financial perspective.

Your sole objective of an interview then is to be in a position of choice – to be offered the role.

This chapter will demonstrate how you can dramatically increase your chances of being offered the job. Interview preparation is core to our highly-successful reputation as recruiters nationally and internationally. Its innovative approach challenges conventional advice. Its new, fresh approach redefines the interview. Your positive, successful performance will create a positive, successful outcome. I have prepared many thousands of candidates for interviews and this is one of my particular specialisms.

I have developed an interview format based on my unique combination of experience as a career coach, recruitment consultant and headhunter. I visit clients, find out their needs and relay that information to candidates. Whilst each role and candidate is unique, I have developed an **Interview Profiler**, which ensures that candidates present themselves confidently, positively and articulately.

What is an interview?

Most candidates envisage interviews primarily as a test or examination. In terms of feedback, it is not uncommon for a candidate to be asked by a friend, 'How well did you do?' and the answer to be, 'I think I did well. I think I answered all the questions,' or 'I don't know. I was not able to answer some questions.' In this instance, the interview was viewed as a knowledge-based exercise, a question and answer scenario rather like a quiz – the more questions you answer correctly the better you are judged.

Importantly, and right at the outset, we need to redefine the role of an interview. Contrary to what you might envisage, an interview is an opportunity to perform rather than simply to be tested.

As a candidate, it can be difficult to know what preparations to make for an interview as there are so many aspects of the event that are unpredictable.

- How do I break the ice?
- Should I try and establish a rapport with the interviewer?
- What sort of person is the interviewer?
- Are they quiet, shy, friendly or aggressive?
- What mood will they be in?
- I want to come across as positive and confident, but not arrogant and pompous – how do I balance those factors in my presentation?
- I don't think I know enough about the job! I hope they don't ask me too many questions.
- I have looked at the website, but it does not help much in terms of this role.
- If there is an interview panel, which person should be the focus of my answers?

Your Interview Profiler

Your Interview Profiler is designed to ensure that candidates give the most positive and articulate account of their skills. It changes the emphasis from a question/answer interaction to the interviewee making a presentation about their relevant skills and creating a positive profile.

The challenge I had was the following: I was sending candidates throughout the world to Bahrain, Paris, London, Geneva, Barbados, Lagos, Munich, Burkina Faso, Rotterdam and Düsseldorf to meet strangers whom, in terms of personality mood and values, candidates could not gauge or anticipate and where they had to selectively talk about the part of their working life that they thought was most relevant to the situation.

The candidate cannot properly prepare for a situation where the parameters are so disparate. However, what the candidate can do is prepare and present a powerful synopsis of their skills that would impress any audience. Integrate this format into interview dialogue and interaction and you will see at first hand the benefit, relevance and power of Your Interview Profiler.

As a recruitment consultant I use this method to prepare all my candidates for client interviews. As a career coach, I use this profiler to instruct all my clients in the art of interview preparation – senior executives on external interview or internal appraisal, MBA students returning to India, China, Africa and Europe. It works for panel interviews and it works when you have multiple interviews for different jobs and are wondering how to adjust your style to each interview. It works cross-culturally. It is not country specific; it is not role specific. It is always **you** specific.

Your strengths

As a prelude to developing a powerful presentation of your personality, you must answer the question:

'What are my particular strengths and how have they worked for me in the past?'

You will choose your strengths from the descriptive lexicons in Chapter 1.

A key output of this process is the identification of your four most character defining and commercially relevant strengths, and the subsequent creation of Your Interview Profiler that directs you to align each of these strengths with two brief, descriptive and, where possible, quantifiable examples of how they have manifested themselves in your working life to date.

Your choice of strengths will depend on the circumstances in which you are applying them.

If you are preparing for a general interview or one where you are not clear about the job requirements, then choose the four strengths that generally best describe your personality.

If you are aware of the job description and have a clear understanding of the soft skills required, then you should choose and elaborate on those particular skills that are most relevant to the job. For example, if you are preparing for a sales type role, then goal orientated, persuasive, good communicator and decisive would be complimentary and focused choices of strengths.

If you are preparing for a technical interview involving IT, accounting or banking, then analytical, organised, good under pressure and works independently might be personality characteristics that would naturally complement this type of work environment.

Compiling Your Interview Profiler

This is always a motivational and exciting journey of self-discovery. This is all about you, your strengths, your achievements. This is a time for you to evaluate and reflect on your achievements and your unique balance of personality (soft skills) and your experience to date, both academic and work (technical skills). Start the evaluation process and discover what unique talents and experiences you have to offer your next employer.

So let's recap. Your Interview Profiler is a template featuring four of your personality characteristics. Each characteristic is supported, confirmed and endorsed by two examples from your CV.

Practice:

1 Choose your four dominant strengths from your descriptive personality lexicon in Chapter 1.

2 Indicate these four strengths, together with sub-topics. The sub-topics are 'anchors' that will help you to define your strengths more clearly.

3 Always give examples that demonstrate how your strengths benefited your employer. Be brief, specific and quantify the benefits where possible. For each strength, reflect on your experience to date and choose two examples that will endorse (prove) this skill.

At the end of this exercise, you will have a powerful interview technique that you can use for all interview situations.

To illustrate its utility, an example of Your Interview Profiler has been compiled below for a Creative Manager on interview for a Design Manager's role.

Your Interview Profiler

1st strength: Examples: A) Presentations B) Department staff

Communication

A) Presentations

> In my current role, I make presentations to Directors of large advertising agencies and to Senior Executives within FMCG multiples.

B) Department staff

> My own department of 26 staff comprises designers and highly-commercial staff, and I successfully get the disparate teams together to work effectively and collaboratively.

2nd strength: Examples: A) New designs B) Run studio

Creative

A) New designs

> I have been responsible for product and packaging designs that have been accepted by the client in a project worth £5 million.

B) Run studio

> I manage a studio of 7 designers, which means training, mentoring and promoting new creative ideas and design skills.

Your Interview Profiler continued...

3rd strength: Examples: A) Manage projects B) Part-time MA

Organised

A) Manage projects

> I currently manage 10 different projects ranging in value from £300k to £7 million. Good organisation and a highly-structured approach to critical path management for all projects, which have separate timescales and content, is vital for successful execution and delivery.

B) Part-time MA

> Two years ago I completed an MA whilst working full time. Successfully managing the priorities was vital.

4th strength: Examples: A) Keep to budgets B) Increased profit by 10%

Commercial

A) Keep to budgets

> I am involved in the formulation of my department's budget with the main Board. In the last 3 years I have never exceeded the budget.

B) Increased profit by 10%

> I have also consistently increased profits, frequently exceeding the target by over 10%.

Example

Your strong, relevant and contextual answers ensure that you create a positive, powerful impression. Thus, dramatically increasing your chances of being offered the role.

Let me give you a further example: If I were developing my own Interview Profiler, I might choose Communicator as one of my strengths and use the following two endorsements:

Good communicator | Examples: A) Stakeholders B) MBA students

A) Different industry stakeholders

> I believe I have strong communication skills as I must engage with Senior Directors across many industries and activities such as oil, finance, retail and IT. Each activity has a different dynamic and culture.

B) Coaching MBA students

> I also coach MBA full-time cohorts from leading universities. Each cohort will have at least 15 different nationalities. This cultural mix means I must communicate and coach in sympathy with each student's culture and personality. I have received over 95 per cent positive feedback.

I have chosen Communicator as a dominant skill choice and endorsed the skill with two real examples. Replicate this format four times, and you will have developed a powerful and relevant Interview Profiler.

Your Interview Profiler provides you with a hard-wired framework on which to focus the discussion of your traits and past experiences during interviews. You will feel more confident, speak with more clarity and do yourself full justice at interview, having familiarised yourself with and internalised Your Interview Profiler prior to interview. Your performance will be more competent, confident and successful, and you will no longer leave an interview with the feeling that you might have neglected to mention any unique selling points.

You will no longer feel: 'I'm not sure how I got on'; 'I'm not sure if I answered the questions correctly'; 'I am not really sure what they were looking for'. Rather, you will be sure: 'I did my best. I presented myself positively and supported my points. My presentation was well prepared.'

You have now developed a presentation about your dominant skills and given examples of how you achieved and practised these skills. Practise delivering this as you would a public speech. It works. It gives you a structure to present yourself to your potential employer.

The interviewer can only make a judgement based on what you say and how you say it. Be proactive. Sitting quietly waiting for a question is too passive and will not give you the opportunity to platform positively.

Using Your Interview Profiler in the interview

You can now use Your Interview Profiler to perform at your best on interview. For example:

Question: 'How do you think you will cope with aggressive clients?'

Answer: 'I believe I am a strong communicator. When I worked in customer support, there were complaints from dissatisfied customers. I received the highest number of compliments from clients for dealing with their problems. When I was leading the debating team at university, the environment was competitive and aggressive. I coached our team to deal with truculent behaviours and how to use humour to deflate a contentious argument. So, I believe I have the skills to deal effectively with difficult clients.'

To adopt the Interview Profiler method requires a radical rethink on the optimum format for interviews. In contrast to the autobiographic style, this method concentrates on you, in other words, your personality. This benefits you by allowing you to articulate your strengths and it benefits the employer as it provides a more useful and transparent means of assessing your suitability.

Remember, from an employer's perspective, the candidate is being assessed for a role that will be new to them involving new challenges, new situations, new cultures and it is the candidate's positive personality characteristics and how they articulate them that will determine their interview success.

Using Your Interview Profiler, which highlights your personality characteristics and endorses each characteristic by examples from your previous performance, must therefore constitute the most powerful interview presentation style.

The amazing fact about Your Interview Profiler is its simplicity, adaptability and outstanding success record. It will dramatically increase your chances of being offered the role.

When you are being interviewed, it is normal for the interviewer to volunteer information such as a synopsis of the company and details about the job, its duties and responsibilities. Using Your Interview Profiler, you are volunteering details about yourself so that the interviewer can make a judgement and compare you and the job.

The most difficult question you could be asked on interview is: 'Tell me about your personality.' This verbally bowls most people out and leads to one or two fairly sparse monosyllabic statements. This reaction is totally understandable, though logically it is a question we should be experts at answering. Our personality is something we rarely talk about or describe in isolation. Yet, we must identify and talk about it as personality traits and strengths are fundamental to our success at work. The sequence of formatting, adopting and presenting Your Interview Profiler is challenging to describe. Ideally, it requires one-to-one coaching sessions and hence I have used different scenarios to ensure you grasp the fundamentals.

I shall conclude my description with a challenge.

Practice:

You are one of 10 candidates who must give a 30-minute presentation about yourself to a panel of three interviewers. You are not briefed about the role and your presentation will be interrupted by questions from the panel.

To prepare for this challenge, you must focus on your personality, your experience and give examples of why you think you have a successful track record to date. This emphasis on you as the prime focus, rather than the role, is the fundamental strength and success of Your Interview Profiler.

This advanced format supersedes the more traditional autobiographic descriptive-based style, whereby you simply describe chronologically your past experiences. Adopt this unique approach and you will dramatically increase your success ratio of interview to job offers.

Chapter 4 Your Work Profile

Imagine you are successful at your role. Your employer rewards you well financially with generous salary rises and arbitrary bonuses. You have been promoted frequently and there is a steady flow of those ego-enhancing headhunt calls offering big salaries and exciting challenges. In terms of performance, you are very successful at 'doing the job'.

This chapter will coach you on how to achieve this goal.

Each individual's circumstances are unique. Your skills, personality and aspirations are unique.

You may be taking up a new role with the company you have been with for some years, or it may be a new role with new people or a new market or a new organisation. Whatever the scenario, you will find the following helpful. The advice is based on my experience of coaching for performance improvement. Facilitating, instructing and coaching candidates on how best to apply their skills and talents is rewarding when the transparent outcome is always the achievement of greater success and higher goals.

The desire to improve is a universal aspiration and the will to act on this desire normally replicates an ambitious, successful candidate. To improve, you must acknowledge that you can do better. To improve also means you are receptive in terms of learning and listening to new recommendations, and the corollary to these characteristics is a candidate who is flexible, adaptable and continually enhances their progress in terms of performance improvement.

The work environment is never static. It is dynamic, fast moving, exciting and challenging, and to keep in step it is logical that successful candidates will invest training time to ensure that they recognise and positively manage the change factors.

I have adopted these important factors in my recommendations. The focus is on your strengths and their application. 'How can I be more reactive, more adaptable – personal skills that are critical in today's globally-influenced employment market?' Identifying your individual and, of course, unique corporate work profile, will enable you to know your strengths, avoid your weaknesses and improve your performance.

Your personality at work

There are three essential categories of interaction that take place in a corporate environment:

1 *Communicating one-to-one when dealing with colleagues and clients.*

2 *Communicating your skills at external interviews and internal appraisals.*

3 *Communicating in groups at meetings, internally and with clients.*

You will have learned how to communicate effectively on a one-to-one basis in Chapter 1, when you will have identified your personality type and its subsequent interactive style. Chapter 3 concentrates exclusively on interview technique for external and internal appraisals. This chapter will coach you on how to perform more successfully in work situations and group discussions.

You will find this session instructional and the content can be applied to all work situations – there are no exceptions.

Usually, we attend meetings on an 'ad hoc' basis and our engagement is determined by 'going with the flow'.

Our opinion of the meeting will vary from boring and inconclusive to interesting and dynamic, from contentious and argumentative to friendly and co-operative.

Our coaching format will ensure that you personally give an impressive and positive performance, whatever the general tone and management.

Group interaction: The ABCD axis – a model for the engagement of individuals in group meetings.

Meetings

This is a fascinating coaching session and one from which you can gain real personal benefit. You will, throughout your working life, attend meetings and you may attend committee meetings as part of your social commitments. The meetings will vary enormously. They will be formal, informal, exciting, boring, dynamic, mundane, decisive, inconclusive, interesting, brief and far too long. And depending on the Chair, the subject and the participants, the tone will be equally variable from lively, flat, friendly, co-operative to truculent, aggressive, contentious and inconclusive.

Anticipating and preparing for the dynamic format and tone of any meeting is difficult. What you can do definitively and effectively is to train yourself to make an influencing and successful contribution to group discussions in a way that you will be regarded as a competent participant. You will gain credibility and respect amongst your colleagues and you will be perceived as a positive contributor in meetings – the one who always asks the salient questions, whose opinions and advice are highly relevant and whose recommendations are always helpful and constructive.

Look at the figure on page 93, which represents participants attending a work meeting. Which role model best describes your normal behaviour?

According to the ABCD axis, a participant's level of engagement is defined as follows:

- **A** is representative of the over-active participant who talks too much, frequently has poor listening skills and verbally rambles from the point of discussion.

- **B** is representative of the active participant who positively and actively engages in the meeting and is a lively, interesting member of the group.

- **C** is representative of the structured participant who lacks the animation and spontaneity of the active participant, but engages purposefully and productively in the group through calculated and quality contributions that are always relevant and to the point. They tend to be extremely good listeners.

- **D** is representative of the quiet participant who rarely interacts in a group meeting, only making occasional verbal forays.

Clearly, there are many factors that dictate the nature of your participation in a group meeting: your persona type, your role at the meeting, your familiarity with the discussion, and how senior or junior you are in relation to the other participants.

The active and structured participants are positive contributors to group discussions and my objective is to coach you to ensure that you belong to one of these categories.

I would describe the active type as frequently engaging with discussion, and doing so positively, relevantly and constructively. I would attribute a similar performance to the structured type who behaviourally is also a successful participant. By comparison, they engage less frequently but when they do their opinions and commentary are valued.

A skill of many successful executives is their ability to develop and steer positive and productive discussion and to encourage the quiet type to be more participatory.

Most of us at some stage have taken part in meetings and, whether through shyness or just plainly 'can't think of anything to say', have made no contribution and did not feel happy about it.

Others may feel that they talk far too much at a meeting and didn't enjoy the reprimand from the Chair to 'Let someone else have a chance to speak'. The reaction to such a veiled criticism is normally to stay quiet deliberately and not take any further part, or to put it in the vernacular – to sulk.

When we take part in meetings we can describe our engagement or what we say as an opinion, a question or a comment and spontaneously we normally use a combination of all three. When we are coaching different personality types to successfully interact at meetings, we demonstrate how to apply these techniques to live situations.

If you are chairing a meeting, you can practise using opinion, questioning and commentary to maximise the collective involvement of the participants and create an environment that is enjoyable, productive, focused and, from the perspective of the agenda, conclusive.

Participation – verbal techniques

To demonstrate the structure and context of these techniques, familiarise yourself with the terminology.

Goal – group

To discuss and debate the agenda to arrive at goals that are the result of the intellectual input of the group.

Goal – self

To act as facilitator, identifying common denominators and building and promoting a collaborative discussion.

Opinion

We are familiar with the approach of someone we would describe as being opinionated: 'I think…, I know…, I disagree…' I discourage this type of participation and encourage a more objective approach, expressing opinion through the impersonal methods: 'Should we consider…? How important do we think…? Some parties might disagree and believe that…' Expressing your opinion in the third person encourages collaborative discussion and a more encouraging democratic and explanatory platform. Practise and adopt this style.

Question

Adopt a similar approach as outlined in opinion above. Endeavour to focus your question on the group rather than an individual: 'To what extent is it important? Should we omit the issue of…? Have we sufficiently justified…?' This encourages the group to engage with your questions rather than you and promotes more qualitative debate.

Commentary

The commentary method is similar to opinion and question, whereby you identify relevant points and make positive endorsements as to their significance and compatibility. This is an effective style of participation. Identify points made that are highly relevant to the agenda and encourage development:

- 'That is a very interesting point, which adds a new dimension to strategic global determination. Perhaps we should discuss its implications in terms of…'

- *'The point Sarah made on critical path analysis endorses David's theory on the optimum method. We could also effectively apply...'*

Practise and adopt these styles, applying them singularly and interactively, and you will be a very productive participant at any meeting. This style gives you entry points – you don't have to wait for that big ego question or posing statement. You may note the absence of judgemental confrontational statements. 'That's right! That's wrong! That's irrelevant! I totally disagree!' – a provocative style that blocks debate and is not intellectually rigorous.

The first coaching stage is to refer to the description of your personality type, which you have identified in Chapter 1, and I shall then describe your particular personality behaviour as a participant or Chair of a meeting. Ad hoc meetings tend to be less successful than those where there is a clear and planned focus and direction as to its structure and objectives, but using your personality strengths and my interactive model, you can successfully participate, whatever the circumstances.

Participation – preparation

These are the main factors you should know before attending any meeting. You may have to consult different colleagues to ascertain the information. If the meeting is well organised, then the pre-briefing will be clear and easily obtainable. 'Difficult to find' information will not inspire confidence and indicates a potentially poor outcome. When you are aware of a meeting, you should request the following information from colleagues or your manager by email or phone (remember preparation is key and the trait of a successful and focused executive):

- Time, duration and location.
- Your role and potential contribution.
- Preparation – references, pre-reading, research.
- Objectives and goals.
- Materials.
- Members attending.
- Agenda composition and dominant issues.

When you are taking part, you should '**TAG**' the discussion as an ongoing task:

- **T – be aware of Time.**

- **A – refer constantly to your Agenda.**

- **G – always keep Goals in sight.**

This will help you to keep your contribution focused and relevant.

You can engage with the group by opinion, question and commentary, and you should use a combination of these basic formats to engage with the conversation.

The Analyst, for example, may feel that they should only talk when there is something new to say. However, they can enter the discussion powerfully through commentary: 'David's point of using historic data which Sarah has formulated sounds sensible. Could that be the best path to follow to reach a provisional figure for this meeting?' – a positive contribution using a collaborative style, respecting others' views, contextually placing them and making a conclusive commentary.

Many senior executives will encourage this democratic technique to ensure that they get the best from the participants and reach successful conclusions. Using these techniques discourages participants and Chairpersons from adopting autocratic and bullying positions to canvass and implement their selfish views. The collaborative technique is most frequently adopted by Managing Directors when they are conducting Board meetings for large multinational organisations.

The agenda may include the ratification of the Report and Accounts, Compliance Reviews, Mergers, Acquisitions and Divestment Reports, Shareholders' and Stakeholders' Interest, Performance Reviews, Marketing Strategy – the list is endless. It is an extraordinary feat of communication when Managing Directors and Chairpersons can tactically and definitively bring such meetings to collective and collaborative conclusion, when you consider that the Board will consist of Directors with international reputations as experts in their field and who will only respect democratic and positive leadership.

A key point here is not to feel that you must contribute something new or say something that sounds important – verbal posturing is not necessary.

Practise active engagement at your next meeting using opinion, question and commentary and you will be surprised at the positive reaction it promotes – all part of developing a successful work profile and an excellent skill for 'doing the job'.

Knowing your personality type and understanding how that relates to you being in charge or being a member of a meeting is insightful, and offers a platform to apply the verbal engagement techniques. At this stage, you will have already identified your personality type and strengths. In the next section, I will demonstrate how you can apply that knowledge to your role in meetings

The Supporter – chairing a meeting

The Supporter will enjoy this role, especially when there is no conflict. They will find it difficult to manage 'personality clashes' as their spontaneous inclination is to develop harmonious relationships and collaboration amongst all parties.

When chairing a meeting, the Supporter should actively encourage the participants to focus on the objectives and agenda. They should lead, control and manage discussions through prompts, endorsing commentary and contributions that are agenda relevant.

Focusing predominately on content rather than personalities will help curtail 'verbal ramblings' and ensure that the meeting concludes positively, having successfully achieved its objectives.

The Supporter – in a meeting

The Supporter should endeavour to focus on the objectives and agenda, concentrating on the points made rather than the people making them. The Supporter has strong people skills and will therefore have a tendency to prejudge comments in accordance with who made them. They must depersonalise conversations. When the Supporter remains task focused, they will make strong positive contributions and play a pivotal role in productively gelling discussions in group meetings. They have a popular persona that creates a tendency of agreement rather than argument – a positive influential contributor.

The Influencer – chairing a meeting

Articulate, friendly, talkative, positive, cheerful – this is the normal persona the Influencer will project to the group members.

The Influencer must manage their own participation and be careful not to constantly 'hog the limelight'. They are good at managing personality clashes. They have a wonderful propensity to develop and encourage positive discussion and ensure that each member has the opportunity to participate.

The Influencer must see themselves in a steerage role and curtail verbal over-indulgence on their part. When focusing exclusively on the agenda and the objectives, and recognising that chairing a meeting is an exciting challenge, then the Influencer can be a Chair par excellence.

The Influencer – in a meeting

The Influencer loves verbal engagement in all its forms – opinion, argument and commentary. They are active and popular participants and it is more in their nature to endorse points made than to take a disagreeable or argumentative stance. They must be prepared to accept criticism. Their strong ego means there is a strong inclination to be defensive of their own opinion.

The Influencer must manage their contributions, ensuring that they are not excessive or irrelevant and the points made not too verbally elongated. This is a personality type with the propensity to be an excellent participant.

The Creative – chairing a meeting

The Creative is predominately task focused and is, therefore, competent at chairing meetings as they will concentrate on the agenda. They have an active 'let's go' mentality and will ensure that the meeting fulfils its objectives within the agreed time. There is a tendency for them to 'shout down' what they consider to be irrelevant points, if their creative argument is challenged, and thereby alienate participants from the discussion. The Creative should conscientiously adopt a diplomatic style, however alien to their normal persona, and be sympathetic to different personality types.

The objective of the Chair is to encourage all participants to positively participate and that strategy, complemented by their natural ability to focus on the goals, will enable the Creative to successfully manage group meetings.

The Creative – in a meeting

The Creative is dynamic and proactive and may have to practise tolerance and patience in meetings that they consider are rambling off the point or are poorly led.

The Creative is a naturally positive participant in group discussions and will make contributions that are relevant, constructive and innovative. They will role reverse in terms of time. Chairing a meeting, they will have a strong time focus but, as a participant, they will tend to disregard time limits and concentrate on the agenda, particularly if the conversation is exciting and challenging. The Creative gets bored easily if the meeting is poorly managed.

The Analyst – chairing a meeting

The Analyst is naturally task focused and will adhere strongly to the agenda and objectives of the meeting. They may have difficulty curtailing the verbally over-enthusiastic Influencer, as this requires a person-to-person engagement rather than a task-focused engagement.

To manage these typical scenarios, the Analyst will have to constantly refer the participants to the agenda, objectives and agreed time allocation. The Analyst is structured and methodical in their management style. 'Blue sky thinking' or 'brain storming' are considered more esoteric thought processes and, as these processes are without a logical base, they are considered time wasting and non-productive. Analysts are strong at chairing meetings, but participants should not expect any radical conclusions or off the wall ideas.

The Analyst – in a meeting

'Quiet, thoughtful, contemplative, doesn't say much,' is how the other members might describe the Analyst. The Analyst engages when they believe there is something relevant to say and a point in saying it.

To participate more actively the Analyst should refer to my coaching recommendations and use the opinion/commentary techniques for positive engagement (see pages 96–97). Having implemented the coaching recommendations, the Analyst will prove to be a vital, structured and productive participant in group meeting sessions.

In summary

Review the advice pertaining to your personality type and understand how to engage positively during meetings. Adopt the TAG discipline and practise your participation using the opinion, question and commentary methods. When you integrate all three factors, you will have the skills and confidence to make a significant contribution to any group discussion.

Progress review meetings – annual appraisals

To gain the most benefit from your job, it is important to know how well you are performing in terms of what is expected of you. Firstly, list your normal duties and responsibilities. Then, note those activities that you regard as not productive and list new responsibilities that you would like to add to your role.

Arrange a review meeting with your manager. It is important, firstly, to establish what your manager considers to be your main duties and responsibilities. Discuss your recommendations and send a summary of the meeting, outlining the new agreed parameters. Arrange a review meeting every six months.

There are many benefits from this regular formal interaction. It will help your manager in the performance of their role. There will be a link and crossover in your duties and responsibilities and the meeting will add a new focus. It will elevate your status. Requesting review meetings indicates an ambitious and conscientious employee.

These meetings are particularly beneficial when you start a new role. It will help you to settle in more quickly. 'But that was not in the job description,' is a common plea by candidates in a new job. Meet your manager as soon as possible to gain a clear outline of your role. You can ascertain the aspects that are prescriptive and those activities that require your own initiative. This will give you a clear benchmark to measure your own performance.

Frequently, when candidates join a new organisation their expectations are high and they can be disappointed and demotivated when colleagues appear non-cooperative and unfriendly – we know from personality profiling that the Supporter and Influencer will be highly sensitive to the working atmosphere. When you have discussed and agreed your role parameters and goals, you will have a well-defined measure of your performance and you will be less susceptible to, or influenced by, peripheral issues such as atmosphere or work environment.

The work environment is demanding and change is not viewed as a separate influencing factor, but rather as an endemic phenomenon. Globalisation has increased competitiveness and put more pressure on margins. On the one hand, this speeding up has created a more dynamic, exciting and challenging commercial climate but, on the other hand, it means employers have higher expectation levels in terms of staff output. A review meeting will ensure you understand and meet yours.

There is more to know…

Now, you should have a deeper contextual understanding of your personality and your particular strengths. Therefore, you can be more selective in your decision making and planning. You are better at matching contrasting behaviours to a type, rather than judging them negatively, because it is not compliant with your personality. You are more tolerant, better informed and feel more positive and proud of your special skills and talents.

From a practical perspective, you have learned how to positively manage the important stages of your career with clear coaching signposts.

As an addendum to *Your Lowe Profile*, I have included additional topics in the appendices. I have identified topics in which readers have demonstrated a particular interest in terms of more knowledge and self-improvement. The topics may not usually be considered core to career management, but they can greatly enhance personal development.

Listening skills, identifying stress, conducting successful interviews and personal goal setting can be an adjunct to career management and fascinating topics for examination and discussion.

Appendices

Listening skills

Listening skills are difficult to write about and coaching on this topic can only really be conducted on a one-to-one basis. However, you may find a description of our structure useful. The best technique for self-improvement is to identify trends in other people.

For example, the people who talk too much are not inclined to be self-critical and will defend any threat of criticism, giving what they consider to be a rational justification. However, they can recognise talkativeness in others when the other party does not give them the opportunity to express their own convoluted opinion! Developing strong listening skills is critical for my role as headhunter and coach. If I am to make an expert assessment of a candidate's or client's personality, I must create an atmosphere in which they can freely express themselves. It is a skill I am constantly endeavoring to refine and improve.

We classify listening techniques in two forms:

1 Parallel.

2 Tangent.

Parallel describes a positive listening skill, when your thoughts and expressions are parallel or in harmony with the other party.

Tangent listening describes a negative or poor listening style, frequently making remarks that are at a tangent to the other party's conversation point. For example:

'I had a bad journey into work today. My train was an hour late.'

A tangent listener would reply, 'Yes, and when I went to Leeds three weeks ago my train was an hour late.' A remark that is of no interest to the other party.

A good listener might have responded, 'Did it disrupt your day? Did you have any early meetings planned?' Or, 'Is it often late?' Parallel listening can be a useful technique for interviews whereby it can be applied to promote better interaction and deal with the problem of 'What questions should I ask?'

Metaphorically, we say that the parallel listener runs verbally with and alongside the other party. Asking for elaboration and clarification is effective during interviews.

Good listening is not a passive mode. It is an active achievement. How often do we use good listening as a compliment? 'They are a good listener.'

Apply good listening skills like this at interviews.

Talking to interviewer:

'You mentioned that multitasking is a key part of the role, can you nominate the various tasks?'

'The job description describes the role as challenging, in what way is it challenging?'

'Data analysis is a key component of the role, how is the data sourced, what is its composition and what is the method of analysis?'

'Communication skills are critical to the role, is that internal or external and who are the audiences?'

'What are the particular challenges or difficulties of this role that may not be obvious from the job description?'

This powerful interactive and engaging dialogue on behalf of the interviewee will elevate their status from the interviewer's perspective. Quality questioning can reflect a quality candidate.

Good listeners are receptive to training and advice. Their mentality is such that training assists them in terms of improvement and development. Dispositionally, the good listener engages on a third-party basis. They talk away from themselves and generally don't refer to themselves. The reference 'I' is seldom used.

The weak listener will normally just converse for their own gratification, not really thinking, 'Are these people interested in what I am saying?' Their conversation will frequently be self-centred and never thought reflective. 'Am I boring you?' would not be a question in the forefront of their mind. They tend to have 'an answer for everything' and are an expert in many subjects. If criticised, they will defend their position. Not having a receptive mentality means they are difficult to train or coach.

Relating listening skills to the four personality types

The Supporter

The Supporter is a good listener and will react in sympathy with their company. In other words, if they are in the company of the Influencer, they will do the listening or, if they are in the company of the Analyst, they will do the talking. The Supporter is a people person and therefore much of their conversations will be people centric. Sympathy and unselfishness are the Supporter's traits and they will demonstrate this emphasis in their people interactions. The Supporter will be reactive and quiet in the company of a verbally truculent person. To interact, they must depersonalise the conversation and engage on a non-people basis.

The Influencer

The Influencer is a poor listener. The fact that we describe the Influencer as articulate, a persuader and good at business development means that they will not have a good listening style. Despite their prominent ego, the Influencer should not consider the poor listening tag as a criticism. Good listening and poor listening styles are dichotomous.

The Influencer must work hard at improvement and endeavour to adopt the parallel listening method as described. The Influencer can practise by omitting the 'I' in conversation, not being opinionated and introducing commentary, 'That's interesting and how did you…?' We all have friends whom we would like to phone to ask for some information, but wonder if we have that much spare time to listen to a self-indulgent verbal presentation.

The Creative

The Creative has a good listening style. They engage in active conversation, which normally is unselfish in its content. They are not political people and can engage with many subjects. Their creative mind means they explore new perspectives and enjoy lively interactions. Conversationally fast and alert, yet argumentative if the need arises aptly describes their personality. A Creative is a good listener with a flexible adaptive style.

The Analyst

The Analyst is a good listener and their platform for conversation will be factual and relational. Small talk is not part of their verbal repertoire. The Analyst can be too reclusive in conversation and should engage the commentary method (pages 96–97) when they are a participant at meetings. The elaboration/explanation style as explained earlier is useful for the Analyst to engage more interactively in one-to-one or group discussions. The Analyst's thought style is retrospective rather than the creation of new conversational topics. The Analyst is a good communicator who can cultivate a more interactive style with experience.

Stress

Most of us experience an element of stress in our working lives. Its intensity will vary and be mainly dependent on the following casual factors: your personality type, your work performance and environment, and your personal circumstances. If you suffer an unexpected and close family bereavement and you are not coping with the pressures of work, then the combination can cause negative stress and greatly influence your performance.

Having a better understanding of what is the most likely factor to cause you stress can help you to recognise the symptoms and alleviate the stress through positive management. It is important to acknowledge that most people do not realise when they are suffering from negative stress. There is a tendency to be defensive when told 'You seem stressed!' 'No, I am not stressed, just very busy at work, nothing I can't cope with.' Stress can cause denial, whereby the person will adopt a defensive attitude and can be difficult to help or speak rationally to regarding their problem. Paradoxically, the answer: 'Do I? That's interesting. I didn't realise it,' is an indication of a person most likely not to be stressed.

It is a shame that stress can cause so much unhappiness in terms of the quality of life, to the point sometimes of causing bad health such as strokes and heart attacks or mental breakdowns, before any remedial action is taken. You will be familiar with the type of comment:

'Since my heart attack I have learned to get my priorities right. I exercise, eat better, enjoy work and all round I am much happier.'

It is a shame that it has taken a catastrophic event to acknowledge the negativity of stress and re-adjust a lifestyle.

The following information may help you to become more alert to situations or circumstances with which you may find difficulty coping. Good advice is always to use external parameters as an indication of stress, rather than your emotive reaction. If you feel the stress is negatively influencing your work performance, then force yourself to discuss the situation with a friend. Disclosure and discussion always help to gain a different perspective on an issue that is worrying you. It can be easy for a third party to recommend another way, a solution, and help you to implement it. This is a satisfying and rewarding part of my role as a coach.

The Supporter and stress

The Supporter is sensitive to the work environment from the people perspective. An aggressive and uncaring atmosphere at work will cause the Supporter stress. An aggressive and uncaring colleague or manager at work will similarly cause stress. The Supporter's natural inclination is to avoid contentious situations rather than confront them, as this is not compliant with their sensitive nature.

Domineering or bullying types will tend to capitalise on the Supporter's rather placatory persona and their behaviour can become more intimidating and stressful. It is difficult to coach a Supporter to deal with these types of extreme behaviour on their own. The most successful approach is to ask for help and discuss the situation with a work colleague or manager. For the situation to be effectively dealt with, it is imperative that the perpetrator is contacted by a third party and made aware of the complaint. In many situations, the person may not be aware of the extent of their intimidating behaviour and most often their response is conciliatory rather than defensive.

In my experience, this type of action generates a personal apology and a cessation of the problem.

The Supporter must be prepared to ask for help and refer to a colleague and follow the colleague's advice to actively confront the situation. Taking no course of action will cause the stress to increase and create a situation of unhappiness and severe pressure on the work and family environment. Ignoring the issue is not an option.

The Influencer and stress

The Influencer thrives on recognition and acknowledgement of achievements. They are generally not prone to stress, as they tend to share their problems with whomever is prepared to listen. This sharing, or to put it more unkindly off-loading, means that problems don't tend to fester in their minds. If a problem arises, the Influencer will not naturally volunteer ownership if it reflects negatively on their reputation.

The Influencer has a large ego and they are protective of their reputation, vehemently defending any misunderstanding that negatively reflects on their personality or achievements. If the Influencer is wrongly accused and the accusation reflects negatively on them, they will 'move verbal mountains' to clarify the situation and rectify the mistake that dents their ego.

Situations where the Influencer is not given due credit for performance or is misunderstood will cause stress. The Influencer plays to win and if there is no benchmark for competitiveness and high profiling, then they will become frustrated and bored. Work that is highly repetitive, monotonous and with no transparent goals for achievement will cause them frustration and the likelihood of changing roles.

Not gaining fair recognition, not being able to perform competitively, being misunderstood, misinterpreted or being falsely accused are the dominant situations that will cause stress to the Influencer. The Influencer can solve their own problems as they are good with people and highly articulate. Therefore, if they do not have the opportunity to perform or clear their name, the Influencer will feel caged and these circumstances would be intolerably stressful.

The Creative and stress

For the Creative, the causal factor for stress will be work related. The Creative has been described as a well-defined personality type with individual traits. The ability to conceptualise is unique. The ability to create is unique to the Creative whether it is a product, a building, a musical composition, fine art, media or graphics, etc. all of which are different, radical and instrumental in the generation of global sales on an unprecedented basis.

Unlike the other personality traits where one can identify a single factor which is the dominant cause of stress, the Creative can be negatively influenced and frustrated by a number of factors. Working in a highly-disorganised environment, unable to use their design and creative abilities and working in a role that lacks challenge or is repetitive and boring, are factors that singularly or collectively will cause the Creative to be stressed. Similarly, an environment where their talents are not appreciated but disregarded and critiqued, will cause the Creative to lose confidence in their abilities and the resultant lack of benefit of their work will cause stress. They are not good at just 'playing the game'. Very often, the only solution is to change role or job, advice which will probably clarify or explain why Creatives change roles more than the average or why they often prefer to work freelance.

The Creative could be coached to adopt a more tolerant attitude, but that approach is more likely to be at the expense of losing some of that positive dynamism that can be the key to their success.

The Analyst and stress

Similar to the Creative, the fact that will cause the most stress to the Analyst will be poor project definition and time. It will be directly work related. The Analyst views the developmental perspective in parallel with the end goal. Their mentality is such that diligently fulfilling the role to a satisfactory technical conclusion is their prime focus – time deadlines can, at times, be secondary considerations.

If there is a time overrun and the cause is outside the control of the Analyst, most often they will not explain this fact. Anything smacking of an excuse is anathema to the Analyst. They do not vehemently defend their corner as the Influencer would do and they do not indulge in blame culture. The Analyst needs to be convinced that the time target is real and that the overrun consequences are also real.

'They always want things done by yesterday. They don't understand the complexity of the content. You can't rush these things. They are complicated and you have to get it right however long it takes.'

This type of typical reaction from the Analyst can cause frustration to those to whom they are reporting and the Analyst will not enjoy the criticism this type of insular reaction will invoke. To alleviate the stress from 'unprovoked negative reactions' (as an Analyst might consider), the Analyst must explain in detail the components of the task in terms of content, complexity parameters and the aspects which, at the early stages, may not be definitive. A car engine may appear to have a particular fault as a result of the noise it is making, but the mechanic will make the proviso that they cannot ascertain the problem until they dismantle the particular parts and examine it personally. The Analyst must explain the process even though it is not their natural remit. This will share the time onus in terms of defining a target and alleviate the stress caused by overrunning the target.

Detailed explanations help to depersonalise situations and by continually briefing colleagues on the progress of the task, the Analyst will fend off those stressful, irate reactions to their apparent lack of time priorities.

Interviewing candidates

If interviewing is something you do not like and feel that you are not particularly good at, then that is a positive or realistic frame of mind on which to build and improve your technique.

If interviewing is something you believe you are good at and if 'I have interviewed lots of people' is your typical suppositional reaction, then you may need coaching in conducting one-to-one assessments. This type of positive reaction can mirror-image an arrogant attitude that portrays a negative learning disposition summarised as, 'I know people. I can sum people up'.

There are three main criteria that influence recruitment interviewing:

1 The personality characteristics of the interviewer.
2 The environment and process.
3 The details of the role.

Interviewing is never a simple exercise of 'summing people up'. It is an exercise in assessing a candidate against the benchmark of a job role. It is circumstantial, situational and contextual. The interviewer is identifying the soft and technical skills of the role and matching these to the candidate. Whilst the interviewer is endeavouring to be as fair and objective as possible, it can be a difficult exercise and depends on the personality type of the interviewer.

The Supporter will tend to concentrate on the soft skills, will endeavour to establish a rapport with the candidate and judge them on emotional criteria, 'I like/dislike' basis. To improve their skills, the Supporter should concentrate on the technical aspects of the role and depersonalise the content of the questions posed.

The Influencer must focus on listening. They will have a tendency to talk too much and therefore not give the interviewee a fair opportunity to ask as well as answer questions. Interviewing is a two-way dialogue, not an interrogation, where both parties can assess each other. When explaining or elaborating on points of the job description, the Influencer should be brief and not offer a verbal dissertation. They must remember that the emphasis is to assess not to perform. They must try not to put too much 'self' into the interview.

The Creative and Analyst normally adopt a balanced interactive interview style. They focus on the technical responsibilities and can dispassionately assess a candidate's objectives. As mentioned earlier, today's employment is predominantly task over people focused and therefore this objective approach replicates today's best interviewing techniques.

'First impressions are everything.'

'I can tell after two minutes whether the candidate is right for the role.'

'It's important to break the ice and chat informally and put the candidate at their ease.'

These views, I am afraid, are not the observations of experienced interviewers and mean that the interviewer is judging from a narrow perspective. The fact that a mathematical modeller presents themselves as a taciturn, verbally reclusive, monosyllabic candidate can be a positive indicator if you are seeking a highly numerate and technical analyst, whilst the energetic, verbose, gregarious candidate may be an excellent fit for that business development role you are seeking to fill.

We know that each situation is very different and the determinants that will influence the outcome are varied. Nevertheless, there are some general pointers that I can recommend and which you can adopt whilst assessing candidates.

Regard historic performance and attitude as a replication and indication of future achievement. The saying, 'Actions speak louder than words' is true in this respect.

'Yes, I did have a lot of time off because I did not find the job very interesting, but I like the sound of this role and I would be much more motivated.'

This would not be regarded as a convincing answer.

Timekeeping is also a crucial indicator. If a candidate is late for interview, they will need a very good excuse. About 3 per cent of my candidates arrive late and most often, when I ask what time they set off, I discover that their time allocation was too intolerant and was based on the assumption that all modes of transport run perfectly on time, without signal failures or traffic jams. Most candidates allow a generous time tolerance for interviews. In my experience, successful applicants are rarely late.

A candidate's voluntary comments are much more valid and reflective of their personality and attitude than those generated by direct questions. You must create an environment and atmosphere where the candidate can make spontaneous comments. Ask open-ended questions that may be tangential to the main point and the candidate's answer will be a more authentic reflection of their personality. Having a very prescriptive list of fixed questions that mirror-image a 'question time' challenge will not allow you to discover the candidate's real interpersonal skills.

Generally speaking, the balance of conversation should be 70/30 in favour of the candidate. Do not conduct stress interviews unless you are highly experienced in managing the outcomes. You may read publications itemising the most difficult questions to be asked and suggesting classic answers; I do not follow this trend. My role as an interviewer is to ascertain if there is a match of skills and not to intimidate or browbeat the candidate with an aggressive inquisition.

In summation, keep the format transparent and adopt a listening style. Let the candidate volunteer their opinion. Identify the skills match and when the interview has ended adhere to your immediate decision. Do not feel that you have to justify your decision with pages of narrative. The brain replicates a powerful processing unit and your decision is therefore informed not spontaneous.

Interviewing is a learning process at which you become more competent and, through experience, progressively skillful.

You can refer to the descriptions of personality and behaviour type which will help you to assess candidates more fairly and contextually. Don't expect the Analyst to be an excellent communicator nor the Influencer to be an expert at quantitative analysis – neither is their forte.

Create a relaxed environment and ask real not posing questions and, surprisingly, your assessment of the candidate, though subjective, will be accurate.

Career goal setting

How helpful career goal setting is will depend on your personality type. The Analyst and the Creative will enjoy goal setting as structured planning is 'in character'. Supporters will take a neutral stance and use it depending on the occasion and circumstance, and particularly if it is recommended by a respected friend or colleague. Influencers are unlikely to spend much time on this exercise and, if they do, they are just as likely to frequently alter their goals or not adhere to them. Influencers are inclined to set ambitious goals that enhance and reflect their ego or, as they would justifiably refer to it, their positive mentality.

Formulating ideas and goals is a highly personal and individual exercise. Some candidates may take notes to interviews, others do not use any notes. I have noticed that Creatives will generally make copious notes during interview or coaching sessions. Analysts will similarly do so, but on a more selective basis. Influencers rarely do and Supporters will make notes if they feel it is expected behaviour. In their private lives, some people rarely write things down; others will constantly make lists and find that without their list they would not function properly. The choice is yours and must be right for you.

Career goal setting can be helpful for candidates who enjoy a structured and organised approach to career management, but the exercise is never right or wrong, only personal.

You are not making a lifetime mission statement. The work environment is changing dynamically and you will need to change and develop your choices, your preferences and skills accordingly. Therefore, goals made now should be for now only, and be adjusted in accordance with your development and market trends.

Identifying personal goals can help to prioritise. It can help to define and balance your work and recreational time.

Goal setting must reflect the future and be flexible, not a written commitment to which you feel obliged to adhere. It is a guide point and indicator. Not fulfilling or meeting goals is not a reflection of failure or lack of commitment; it may be a reflection of your flexibility and adaptability.

Coming soon by the same author...

1 The Winning Partnership: CV and Job Applications

CV – How long should it be? One page, two pages or more? What should you put in and what must be left out? I have read over 100,000 CVs and have developed a simple template that always works. But a CV is never a standalone document. Discover the winning partnership!

2 Interviews: My Worst Nightmare

I have devised a unique template for interview preparation. It redefines an interview as 'an opportunity to perform rather than a situation to be tested'. I use it for all my candidates and at all levels. It works. Feedback – 100% complementary.

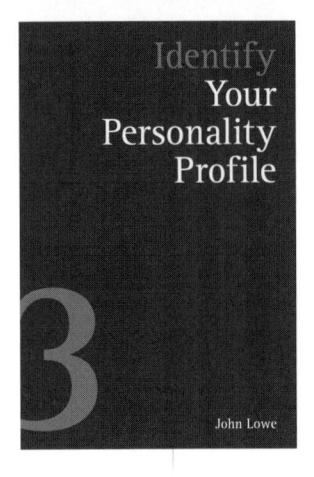

3 Identify Your Personality Profile

'Play to your strengths,' we say. But do we know our real strengths and how crucial they are in the work environment? This self-validation is unique to John Lowe and based on his 20,000 candidate and client interviews. It's unique and foundational to all career coaching.

4 Can I Be An Entrepreneur?

Big topic! Many of us would like to be our own boss. No annual appraisals, no politics, no clock watching, no need for structured career path. OK then, find out how and enjoy the read.

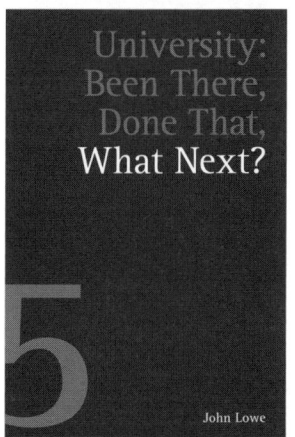

5 University: Been There, Done That, What Next?

Only been in education for the last 17 years? Jobs, careers, which one? How do I apply and how do I know the one which suits me best?

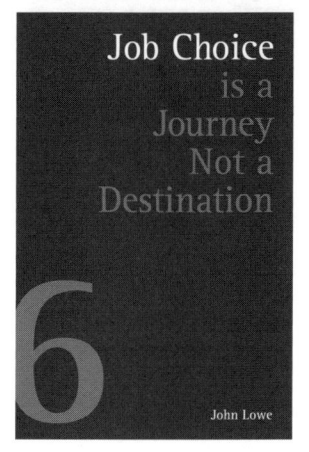

6 Job Choice is a Journey Not a Destination

Today's commercial environment is not structured. Career ladders have rungs missing. Find out why and then your plans will be real and realisable.

7 Surviving Redundancy

Surviving redundancy is more about your attitude and skills and not about recessions and company closures. Surviving redundancy will make you more resilient to global downturns and less fearful of negative trends.

8 Is Extrovert Good or is Introvert Better?

This will change popular thinking. Find out your personality type and learn why your friends and family behave as they do. They may be more normal than you think!

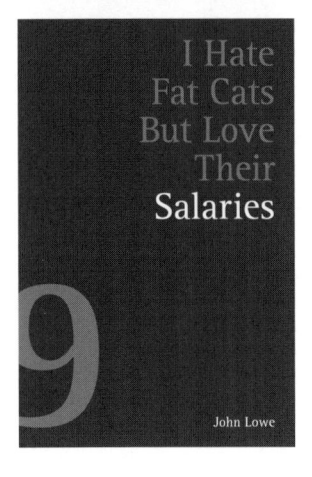

9 I Hate Fat Cats But Love Their Salaries

A review of the ethics of salary and allaying the myth that the highest paid are the highest performers. Pay less and recruit better managers. Find out why and check out your own worth.

10 Am I Stressed?

We all get stressed at some stage and the point of this booklet is to show you how to avoid it if you can and manage it if you can't.

11 How to Have a Gap Year *Every* Year

Can work be play? Does work always have to be a nine to five grind? Find out how to discover your alternatives.